SILVER BULLETS

75 STRAIGHTFORWARD
TIPS TO TAKE YOU TO THE TOP

VINCE POSCENTE

Published by Be Invinceable Group
Dallas, TX
www.beinvinceable.com

Submit all requests for reprinting to:
CornerStone Leadership Institute
P.O. Box 764087
Dallas, TX 75376
888-789-5323

For ordering information or special discounts for bulk purchases, please contact CornerStone Leadership Institute, P.O. Box 764087, Dallas, TX 75376, 888-789-5323.

Design and composition by Greenleaf Book Group LP
Cover design by Greenleaf Book Group LP

ISBN-10: 0-977225-78-X
ISBN-13: 978-0-9772257-8-1

Printed in the United States of America on acid-free paper

06 07 08 09 10 11 12   10 9 8 7 6 5 4 3 2 1

First Edition

TABLE OF CONTENTS

Target   More Money and Results: Skinny, Rich, and Irresistible

Target   Happy Employees, Strong Business: Dead Frogs

Dedicated to my best friend,
wife, and source of inspiration,
Michelle.

 **TARGET**

BIG PERSONAL SUCCESS
DON'T PUSH THE RIVER

1 | DON'T PUSH THE RIVER

Go with the flow. Use your energy wisely. Rest with intention.

If you ever forget who said something, just call it a Chinese proverb. "Don't push the river" is one such proverb. And for what it's worth, what does it really mean?

There are three basic messages inherent in "Don't push the river."

1. **Go with the flow.** This is not about being a helpless cork in the river of life. This refers to an awareness of the natural order of the environment you are in. It is a balance of the instinctual interpretation and a cerebral context. Where is the flow in your job or relationships? How can you maximize your position so that everyone wins?

2. **Use your energy wisely.** It can be tempting to conquer all that stands in your way. With dogged determination and brute force, you can be the victor. A worn-out, bewildered victor. Use the martial arts technique of using the force that faces you to your own advantage.

3. **Rest with intention.** Find the places in the metaphorical river of life to rest. There are eddies where you can recoup your spirits and regain perspective. Rest frequently, and pop back into the flow when you have caught your breath.

2 | UNENCUMBERED THOUGHT

Introduce your positive thinking to unencumbered potential.

Last month I treated myself to a few days of helicopter skiing. To add to the magic of the snow-capped Rocky Mountains of British Columbia, I spent three days hanging out with the operation's owner and founder, Mike Wiegle. Just a few hours with Mike caused a huge epiphany for me . . . one I would like to share with you.

Throughout the ages, many have advised that positive thoughts will create positive outcomes. The power of positive thinking is cliché in the world of motivation. Yet, why do some people succeed with positive thinking and others don't?

Mike Wiegle is a hugely successful entrepreneur. He started a heli-ski operation thirty-five years ago in the middle of nowhere. Nobody would fund him. Today, he runs a multimillion-dollar operation, clients pay over one thousand dollars per day per person, and Mike gets to ski virgin powder every day. Mike Wiegle is sixty-six years old and the only lines on his face are from smiling all the time.

I asked Mike if he ever surprised himself. His answer was nothing short of cliché. He said that his positive thoughts eventually have a positive result. I personally wrestled with his answer, knowing that many people have positive thoughts and few seem to turn them into extraordinary successes. Then the proverbial aha light bulb illuminated my thought.

If at any point your positive thoughts are encumbered by negativity (hidden deep in the subconscious mind) then the positive thought is like a hand pushing water against the flow of a river. Yet, if the hand pushes water in still water, it instantly creates a flow.

Think again about the Chinese saying "Don't push the river." How powerful would your positive thoughts be if you had still waters in your mind? How much more powerful would your thoughts be if you introduced them to the natural flow of a river? How much more quickly would your thoughts manifest extraordinary outcomes if you found the part of the river with maximum flow?

Introduce your positive thinking to unencumbered potential and prepare for two smile lines for all to see . . . for years to come!

3 | BREAK THROUGH THE NEGATIVE CRUST

Undesirable situations are primarily born out of patterns you hold unconsciously.

That last Invinceable Insight may have left many readers asking . . . "But how can I have unencumbered thoughts?" Positive thoughts alone may not break through the thick crust of negative patterns, and we can be left in a world of frustration.

Over the years, you and your environment have been programming your conscious and subconscious mind. You have succeeded in ingraining both patterns that serve you well and others that limit your effectiveness. Each part of your brain works in harmony with the rest to protect and guide you through life. Undesirable situations are primarily born out of patterns you hold unconsciously.

You max-out your credit card and wonder how you got there again. You get in a familiar argument and it all seems futile. You feel your boss holds you back from doing what needs to be done. The list of negative outcomes can be long, and trying to eliminate items on this list can be a perplexing effort. Even though we are gifted with the power of choice, we are often beings of conditioned reflexes. How do we change? How do we get new results? If we are truly "creatures of habit," how can you or I make a change for the better?

There are four ways to change patterns:

- **Instantly.** This is usually associated with hitting rock bottom, a near-death or severe loss situation. The company comes close to bankruptcy and the decision makers make the drastic changes necessary to save the organization. A smoker loses a lung and decides to quit smoking. An alcoholic loses his house, family, and lifestyle and realizes he needs to quit drinking. Yes, the pattern changes, but the change can be arduous and painful.

- **Trial and error.** This is where a vast majority of organizations and people can be found. It's not a bad method. It simply follows our natural tendency to learn by doing and avoid any discomfort. We try, make mistakes, have some wins and move forward.

- **Proactively.** Learning organizations, training programs, individuals committed to personal growth, and people who invest in learning tools are all examples of this less common but more effective way to accelerate positive outcomes. Being proactive builds on the trial and error method of finding your desired outcomes.

- **Consistently Applied Strategy.** C.A.S. is the quickest, most effective, and most efficient way to break through the negative patterns and realize extraordinary outcomes. C.A.S. will not work if you do not have: (1) a clear vision of the future that you want to create, and (2) a maniacal dedication to staying aligned to that vision in thought and action. If you have the vision and dedication, old patterns will disintegrate and disappear. C.A.S. leverages both trial and error and proactive behavior to take a straight line to the vision you lock in on.

To help you or your company hit targets quicker with C.A.S., use gold dots scattered around your house, your office, or anywhere you are to remind you of your vision and ignite the emotional buzz that goes with it. The idea is to first target where you want to go. Then use gold dots as triggers to stay aligned with your vision.

4 | PAINT THE PICTURE

You can get thousands of people aligned with a simple visual.

You can get thousands of people aligned with a simple visual. Do this and your future is bright indeed.

Ray Wierzbicki, senior VP of enterprise at Verizon, leads a few thousand *very* loyal employees through the challenging world of customer service in the telecom world. His goal is to have his employees imagine they come "skipping to work." It appears to work and their culture reflects it.

Paint the right picture and people will follow you most anywhere. Most of the time . . . .

My quick-witted Irish grandmother used to say, "Blow in my ear and I'll follow you anywhere." At age 6, that kind of weirded me out. By age 16 I wondered if it really did work on girls. (Note: As the second clarinet player in the band, standing a towering five feet tall with limited access to my mom's wood-paneled station wagon, I realize now that ear blowing would not compensate for everything, no matter how hard I blew.)

What's with the ear fixation anyway?

Remember in your youth hearing

- "The only thing you should put in your ear is your elbow."

- "Friends, Romans, lend me your ears . . ."

- "God gave you two ears and only one mouth, so zip it and listen."

Anyway . . . paint the picture and you will get people thinking.

Coke did this in the mid '80s when they went through the New Coke disaster. With a full-scale consumer revolt, Coke (with management consultant Jim Crupi, PhD) went back to basics and changed their vision statement to a simple visual: "Put a Coke within reach of every human being on the planet."

Coke just might make it after all.

Business people everywhere, it's time to take it to the next level and brighten our future. Paint the picture.

Let's all skip to work with a beverage in one hand and one elbow in an ear.

5 | **WORK WITHOUT LOVE**

---

*Define what you love in your work right now and
make this your message, your mission, your job.*

Work without love is slavery.

—*Mother Theresa, 1910–1997*

You can hate the paperwork. You can hate the travel. You can even hate your boss. But if you don't love your job, something's wrong. Something needs to change. That change must first come from within.

Loving your job is a question of being part of something for the greater good. What is the greater good that you are a part of?

Steve Jobs, CEO of Apple, gave a speech to graduates at Stanford University and put it this way. "Your work is going to fill a large part of your life, and the only way to be truly satisfied is to do what you believe is great work. And the only way to do great work is to love what you do."

Herb Keller, cofounder of Southwest Airlines, put it another way. "You know, there are plenty of companies where it is acceptable to clock in and clock out each day, making a tiny speck of a mark on the world. But a company like Southwest Airlines has always attracted people who would rather paint a wide, vivid swath. Those are the people who make a positive difference. Those are the people who will take this company, successfully, into the next 34 years. I love them all and they know that."

Work without love is work without a mission. Mother Theresa also said, "My life is my message." The message she sent was one of love. A message that endures.

What is your message? What is your mission? What is your job?

Quitting your job is not the answer. You will only drag the same issues to your next job. Define what you love in your work right now and make this your message, your mission, your job.

6 | YOU HAVE TO LAUGH

Laugh . . . no matter what the outcome is.

Taking on a project has three distinct parts: the planning, the execution, the outcome … the one you didn't expect.

The plan. Put in a waterfall and koi pond in the backyard in the sloping, unusable part of the property. Enjoy the hypnotic sounds of water running down into a serene pool of water.

The execution. Get in way over your head. Buy a book on how to build your own waterfall and believe the part where they say "it's easy." Buy and individually carry sixteen tons (that's thirty-two thousand pounds) of rock. Install a pump/filtration system, fifty feet of underlayment (new word) and liner. Hire workers who don't know anything about waterfalls or the English language, get out and start digging. But the payoff is coming after three weeks of manual labor in temperatures over one hundred degrees Fahrenheit.

The outcome. The moment that you've been waiting for. With the flick of a switch the water will flow, along with the feeling of *I built that.* Drumroll.

As the water starts to cascade down the moss rock slope the whole hypnotic, serene thing is crushed like a peach under a rhinoceros foot.

GranklgrglkrankrankGRANKLGRGLKRANKAGRLNGK. . . .

The neighbor fires up a wood chipper the size of a moving van, making the sound of a jet engine churning up a hundred crescent wrenches. Fargo meets two hundred decibels.

So things might not work out the way you romanticize. You still have to laugh . . . it's the best way to keep your wits about you.

7 | TAKE MY ADVICE, PLEASE, I'M NOT USING IT

The way we act is the way we teach.

Do you ever get the impression that some people are essentially saying, "Take my advice, I'm not using it"?

Yes, we're all human. We slip up. When my son, Max, was four, he tested the boundaries of bad behavior (he must take after his dad). Anyway, he pressed enough buttons that I started to raise my voice (otherwise known as yelling).

Max raised his hand, waved me to eye level, and said in a hushed tone, "You know Daddy, you are teaching me how to be a dad."

Gulp.

At Be Invinceable Group, we talk at length about alignment and peak performance. We write about leadership of the self and making a difference in the world. Thanks to little Yoda-Max we now consistently remind ourselves that the way we act is the way we teach.

Enjoy the journey and keep learning from the slip-ups!

That's advice we like to use.

8| LETTER TO MR. MILLER

*Thank you for the lessons of respect, the love
of learning, boundaries and leadership.*

Dear Mr. Miller,

It has been twenty-eight years since I sat in your phys ed class but your lessons live on.

You taught *respect*. While most teachers maintained control with authoritative and punitive actions, you managed to speak to your students at an entirely different level. You did not preach but you were knowledgeable. You made each lesson an opportunity to grow through self-discovery. As a parent I finally get what you were doing. You respected your students enough to facilitate learning from within.

You taught the *love of learning*. While most teachers thought their job was to teach their students lessons, you were obviously a student yourself. You would hold up books that you had researched the night before. You made it clear that you loved to learn from your students and you were never shy about diving into topics. I know that part of my curious nature was fertilized by your immense love of learning.

You taught *boundaries*. While most teachers used the trappings of a meritocracy as an important life lesson, you taught that boundaries are boundaries. You might remember giving an outline of the year's class schedule. On the first day you made it clear that in the session about what to do in a childbirth emergency, if there was any childish behavior you would cancel the lesson. The week before the class you reiterated this boundary. On the day of the class, as seemed inevitable with seventeen-year-old boys, the immature comments started to fly. To this day I remember how you closed your teaching binder and canceled the lesson. A boundary is a boundary.

You taught *leadership*. While most teachers were leading by command and control, you lead by example. Leadership is defined many different ways. My favorite is a Jim Kouzes quote, "A leader is one who mobilizes others to want struggle for shared aspirations." Mr. Miller, I don't ever remember your lessons as easy. I do remember that you wanted each and every student to stretch. When a student stretched in his personal life you made the group share in the joy. You gave responsibility and allowed us to lead sections of classes. The Latin word for learning by doing is praxis. Through praxis we grew as leaders. With shared aspirations of adulthood we were stronger in your presence.

Mr. Miller, I think of you often and am thankful for the impact you made on my life and the lives of hundreds of students.

Thank you for the lessons of respect, the love of learning, the boundaries, and the leadership.

9| WHAT'S YOUR POSITION BASED ON?

The most courageous journey you can take is the journey within.

I'm a Republican. I'm a Democrat. I'm pro-choice. I'm pro-life.

I'm treading on thin ice . . .

Everyone is entitled to an opinion. But the next time you are at a dinner party or in a lively discussion, instead of voicing yours, sit back and listen to others as they voice theirs.

Ask yourself, what are their opinions based on?

Are they based on

- personal experience?

- a repertoire of research?

- a logical conclusion after years of trial and error?

- an intuitive feeling?

- peer pressure?

- a desire to be part of some movement or community?

- fear?

Later, reflect on your position and what is it based on.

The most courageous journey you can take is the journey within. How far are you willing to journey down this path?

10 | DO YOU THINK OR DO YOU KNOW?

There doesn't seem to be any shortage of opinions and assumptions.

Sara Kathryn was four when she questioned her parents' position.

"Do you think or do you know?" she asked.

Her parents were agog and flummoxed (pretty fancy words for weirded out).

Agog because of the wisdom their obviously gifted child showed. Flummoxed because she hit a nerve. They had stated their position as fact. The truth was, they were really basing their position on a commonly held assumption.

There doesn't seem to be any shortage of opinions and assumptions.

Here, this one should do a number on your brain . . . Parents don't really matter when considering the personality of a child.

I can see the emails now. "You're wrong, Vince." "Are you crazy?" "Do you believe everything you read?" "This is the stupidest article you have ever written!"

Judith Rich Harris wrote a book titled *The Nurture Assumption.* In it she presents an absolutely persuasive argument on virtually every tenet of child development. Entire fields of research in the areas of parental upbringing and genetic endowment are convincingly debunked. This Pulitzer Prize finalist challenges what we take as absolute truth regarding the influence genetics and parenting has with the way children turn out.

Harris uses technical literature from anthropology, cultural history, psychology, and behavioral genetics to support a thesis that peers and genes matter—parents don't.

As food for thought, let me leave you with the following. What's your evaluation of the next sentence?

A child's parents shape or modify the child's personality and character.

"Fact," you say.

Well, Smarty Pants . . . do you think or do you know?

11| SOFT FOCUS: NOT FOR SISSIES

Things are happening so incredibly fast; you will do better by learning how to apply soft focus.

Imagine skiing at 135 miles per hour. What do you focus on?

Do you focus on a bump up ahead, the trees on the left, the best line to take, the position of your hands, the weight over your skis? What particular thing do you focus on with so much changing around you?

In any speed sport, the focus is entirely on nothing and everything all at once. That is soft focus.

In any environment where you find yourself dealing with rapid change, you will be well served to take your focus off one thing or another and use the three tenets of soft focus.

Feel the mojo. For all you linear left-brainers this won't make a lot of sense. Feeling the mojo is about a sense of knowing. It is what golfers know but can't describe. It is what sales people feel but can't predict. Feeling the mojo is less about doing and more about being. When it's right . . . you know! You feel the mojo.

Trust the elephant. If you have read *The Ant and the Elephant*, you know that the elephant is a metaphor for the subconscious mind. The subconscious is the storehouse for everything you know. It is able to process complex information that the conscious mind (the ant) cannot handle at high speeds. Sensory overload is a clear sign the elephantine subconscious has taken over. If you have prepared in advance the elephant is prepared. Let go. Trust the elephant.

Faster, faster, faster becomes slower. Skiing at a hundred miles per hour for the first time is an eye-popping, sphincter-clenching experience. But, ski at a hundred miles per hour a dozen times and you begin to see things you didn't see before. You begin to take in more. The only way to be comfortable at high speed is to repeat until you get jiggy with it (jiggy: an Ebonics word for in sync). Increase your speed in measured amounts and you will eventually slow down what used to feel too fast. Fast becomes slow.

Skiing at 135 miles per hour is much like dealing with the competitive landscape of our corporate world today. Things are happening so incredibly fast; you will do better by learning how to apply soft focus.

12 | BUMP MASTERY

Ignite. Execute. Eclipse.

"At 138.2 miles per hour, on skis, you hit a bump. Your body strains against total chaos. In a nanosecond everything you plan vanishes. You ultimately go from gold medal contention to an athlete struggling with the effects of hitting a bump . . ."

Bumps!

In business, the last five years have been bumpy to say the least. Now is the time for you to get past the bumps and have an extra jump on the competition. What bumps are you dealing with?

- salespeople consistently not hitting their numbers quarter after quarter

- high performers suffocated by "to dos" from corporate
- finding a way for sales to come from more than the top 20 percent of producers
- motivating your sales force to be self-motivated
- the 'pressure cooker' to sell more with smaller budgets and less people

Is this your game plan?

- Make your next annual sales meeting the pivotal point for the next six to eighteen months.
- Build more momentum than the competition does.
- Motivate yourself yet again for a year of more, more, more.
- Deliver on the promises that you made or quotas that were imposed.

How will you follow through on your game plan? In order to take on the year ahead, try an approach that has worked very well for us and our clients.

First, *ignite* with an assignment: Differentiate your approach by changing it from an objective to an assignment. For all us in the forty-plus club, remember the TV show *Mission Impossible*? Each episode, the star heard the tape player announce, "your assignment, should you choose to accept it . . ." The mission was clear and exciting. Ignite your interest and treat your objectives as an assignment.

Second, *execute* with alignment: "Is this aligned?" is the mantra we recommend for all our clients. With a clear and exciting assignment, execute on the plan, ensuring every step you take is consciously aligned.

Third, *eclipse* with improvement: Consistently improving every time you are in the field or in the office will garner visible, quick, and compound rewards. The Japanese call it kaizen. I call it the mindset of a high performer. Eclipse your past performance (even if it is only by 1 percent) and you will eclipse your competition.

While your competition is hitting bumps along the way, you will speed past them leaving a cloud of snow and ice. When you hit bumps yourself, reapply the *ignite, execute,* and *eclipse* approach and carry your momentum through another great year.

13 | JUNGLE JIM

Do your best and you will have no regrets.

"Hello, this is Jungle Jim."

"Hello, Mr. Hunter?"

"Call me Jim."

"Jim, my name is Vince Poscente. I'm twenty-six years old and I have never ski raced before and I would like to compete in the next Olympic Winter Games in France four years from now. I was wondering if you had any advice?"

There was a long pause from "Jungle" Jim Hunter, a medalist in the Olympic Winter Games in Sapporo. Finally the silence was broken and he spoke three words that echo in my mind eighteen years later.

"Have no regrets!"

He paused again and continued. "When it is race day and you know you have done your best . . . you know deep down there was *nothing* more you could have done, then your best is all you can ask for. If you have done your best, know that *your best can be the best in the world!*"

Dear Reader . . . know that these words apply to you too. If you do your best, your best can be the best in the world.

If you are not doing your best, then don't be surprised by the less-than-the-best results you may be experiencing in your life.

If you are manifesting substandard results and *think* you've tried your best, it's time for a self-honesty check. There is likely something more you could do. Do your best and you will have no regrets!

14 | **EXTRA INNINGS**

Are you prepared for extra innings in your pursuits?

In baseball, extra innings usually force the team coach to draw on his pitchers in the bullpen. In business, some projects take more time and money than expected. In life we will live longer than our forefathers did past the traditional retirement age of sixty-five. In families, the kids are leaving home much later in life.

What are you doing to plan for extra innings in your pursuits?

The fun thing about life is that it is so unpredictable. But that doesn't mean that you have to leave everything to chance.

In sports, coaches have contingencies in place. Hockey coaches know to use their fourth line more if the game goes deep into overtime. In basketball, coaches know that some of their top players may foul out. They have some key players ready to come off the bench. In dogsledding . . . well . . . I don't know anything about dogsledding but I'd have a few extra dogs if those Iditarod pranksters moved the finish line an extra hundred miles north.

In business, budgets get blown when unexpected stuff happens. The founder of Kos Pharmaceuticals started his company with a $30 million budget and three years. Nine years and $90 million later the first reps hit the street. Ouch! But the company obviously had reserves (otherwise known as a huge bank vault) to make their investment pay off.

As for life, the president and CEO of AIG Financial Advisors, James R. Cannon, reports that people are likely to live 18.6 years past the traditional retirement age of 65. He is positioning his independent financial advisors to meet a market demand for more retirement dollars than originally planned.

At home, kids are staying longer. These are extra innings for parents good and ready for their kids to leave. It must be hard to say no to a kid who has come back and won't leave. Here are some alternative ways to say "We love you but it's time to scram":

- Change their room into a sewing and Canasta parlor

- Run a significant electrical charge to the fridge door handle

- Join a witness protection program

- Leave Planned Parenthood brochures on your desk with a Post-it note that says "To Do: Check to see how old kids have to be to put them up for adoption."

- All of the above

Are you prepared for extra innings in your pursuits?

Here are three things you can do:

- Have a contingency fund ready for extra innings ($60 million ought to be enough)

- Decide up front that you will quit at a given point in time (Note: the withdraw method doesn't always work)

- Come up with at least six different scenarios that could happen if your pursuit did run longer than expected. Imagine how you would handle each scenario.

15| **THE CONTAGIOUS CONFUSER**

Confusion is a disease to any relationship or organization.

All it takes is one person in a choir to be confused and others get mixed up. Put one hockey player on the ice who doesn't know a play and the team quickly loses control of the puck. Experience one actor messing up his lines and feel an entire theatre squirm in discomfort.

Confusion is a disease to any relationship or organization. Confusion can grow and spread in hideous ways. Here's how to avoid the embarrassment and dysfunction of being the "contagious confuser."

1. **Know thyself.** I have said it before; the most courageous journey a person can take is journey within. Looking for issues within can be frustrating and scary. Frustrating because most dysfunction is hidden in the elephantine subconscious mind. Therefore, solutions can be hard to determine. Scary because

you may realize something about yourself that needs changing. Fear not, there is strength in understanding!

2. **Know thy confines.** When can you innovate and when do you stick to the plan? Practice and consistent communication are the only way to find an effective answer. Fear not, there is control in order!

3. **Know thy bull's-eye.** What is the group target? What do you need to know about each person's objectives and the overall goal? Keep all your actions aligned with the target and trust will be your ally. Fear not, there is power in confidence!

Amen.

16 | DOO-DOO MAGNETS BEGONE

Fixating on the problem is not the solution.

There are people that love problems. These people have many names. My favorite is *doo-doo magnets*. They're addicted to troubles. They find problematic issues irresistible and share their woes with everyone within earshot. Sure, it's natural to turn your attention to something going wrong. But fixating on the problem is not the solution.

There are three kinds of problems, each with its own set of solutions.

1. **Circumstantial problems.** These are the kinds of problems to get past as soon as you can. Examples are getting double-booked, not

finding the right kind of spaghetti sauce, a bad shoe/purse combination, or a rip in your pants just seconds before a speech.

The answer is simple. Look past the problem and immediately focus on the solution. Don't be a poop attractor. It's a problem. Get over it. Leave it behind and march directly towards a resolution (and face the crowd, but don't turn to see the Power Point slide).

2. **Fear-based problems.** In situations that cause anxiety, take a page out of a flight attendant's take-off guide.

"In case of depressurization, oxygen masks will drop down from the overhead bins. Place the plastic cup over your nose and mouth and—get this—"breathe normally."

Breathe normally?

BREATHE NORMALLY?

We are plummeting towards the earth at five hundred miles per hour. Who's planning on breathing normally?

Seriously, most fears are about things that haven't happened. My teenager missed her curfew and she hasn't checked in. I messed up at work and my boss doesn't know yet. The car is making a funny noise and I bet it's the transmission going out. Oh, that hole in the ozone layer is just a fad (and some fears are worth paying attention to).

Obsessing about the problem is only going to hinder clear thinking. Leave that up to the big boom boom hold-er on-er who *likes* to obsess about problems. With fear-based problems the smartest, most efficient thing you can do is immediately plan a way to reach your targeted result. Then take action!

3. **Pain-based problems.** Pain-based problems are the worst.

They present a huge distraction, especially when there is a look-who-done-me-wrong caca cowboy in our midst. We don't need *him* to remind us of the financial pressures, relationship woes, employment issues, or health problems that crop up now and then. Yet pain-based problems need to be addressed immediately. I recommend the following:

- **Acknowledge the problem.** Ignoring the problem is like stuffing it into a drawer and pretending it doesn't exist. It is human nature to avoid problems. It is also human nature to solve problems. Acknowledge the problem and be honest with yourself and others.

- **Isolate the problem.** Isolate the issue and you accelerate a solution. Alcoholics increase their chances of quitting successfully if they check into a rehabilitation center. A problem at work can solved quicker if you retreat to planning conference where 100 percent of your focus is on the issue. Isolate the problem and you have a much better chance at solving it.

- **Chip away at the problem.** The best time to work on a problem is before it happens. The next best time is as soon as you realize there is a problem. The worst time to work on a problem is after it has grown fangs and a nauseous smell. Immediately begin to chip away at the problem and you will see results.

All doo-doo magnets, begone. We've got problems to solve and you're not helping.

17| HOW TO BE YOUR OWN WORST ENEMY

Take yourself seriously.

---

1. Only make statements, ask no questions.
2. Don't question whom you follow.
3. Don't follow your own advice.
4. Give unwelcome advice.
5. Expect others to be a certain way.
6. Find a way to blame anyone or anything but yourself.
7. Take yourself seriously.
8. Don't be serious about following up on your commitments.
9. Commit to promises you cannot keep.
10. Keep being consistently late or missing appointments.
11. Did I miss anything?

 TARGET

DEEP PERSONAL GROWTH

NAKED IN THE MIRROR

18 | NAKED IN THE MIRROR

Your life takes consistent, dedicated attention.

Most of us have been there . . . you walk out of the shower past the mirror and then there is a silent scream of "Arghhhhh! I have to get in shape." (Those of you under twenty-five need to pretend you know what I am talking about.)

Learning the truth in your business or personal life can be much more difficult, since we can hide behind our various protective layers. But when the truth is reflected right back to you, you can decide what needs to change.

Without standing in front of a mirror in your birthday suit, here are three ways to get the truth that may be hidden:

- **Strip down to your values.** The first thing to do is understand what your core values are. What values are nonnegotiable in your life? Compare this list of values to how you are living your life.

- **Look for the lumpy parts.** Coworkers who have the heart to be honest, friends who care enough to tell the truth, siblings who have nothing to lose can all be great sounding boards for stuff you can work on. Here's a tip . . . if you don't ask, they likely won't tell. Take some quiet time, sit face to face, and ask where the lumpy parts in your personality are. (PS . . . If your mouth has to move during this interaction, make sure it is only used to ask clarifying questions.)

- **Take "before" and "after" snapshots.** Imagine the "after" snapshot you want your life to look like. Take inventory of what you have today (the "before" picture). What is not aligned? What needs to change today to get the result you are looking for?

Like your physical fitness, your life takes consistent, dedicated attention. If you keep hiding behind the garments of staying busy and people who tell you what you want to hear, then the truth will elude you. Fulfillment and happiness will too.

19 | MIRROR, MIRROR ON THE WALL . . . HEY, LOOK WHO'S HOLDING YOU BACK (PART 1)

Successful people apply consistent strategies and totally commit to self-improvement.

Who's holding you back? The mirror remains silent. All you see is your face. Hmmm, looks like the mirror has the answer. Apply consistent strategies and change the question to "Who's the most successful of all?"

What do all successful people have in common? They apply consistent strategies and totally commit to self-improvement. Consultant and trainer Stephan Iscoe has some great news: "The miracle of successful living is that the smallest step toward success attracts more success!"

How can you create this miracle in the present and the future? All it takes is an attitude of persistence. So, whether you're trying to diet or succeed in business, here are a few tips that will help you apply consistent strategies.

- **You learn best by doing while remaining flexible.** Remember, the Greek word *praxis,* "to learn while doing."

- **Paint the picture for yourself and others.** When you set a routine, visualize attaining your goal.

- **The process is the goal.** The goal is the process. Success is a journey, not a destination.

- **Develop routines any way you can.** Create habits or routines that work for you and remain consistent in your efforts.

- **Prepare yourself to act quickly, while remaining focused on the solution.** With today's rapid pace of change, if you don't focus on a solution and act quickly, you'll be left far behind.

It takes twenty-one days, on the average, to change a habit. Really, there's nothing special about that number, unless you're playing blackjack. Social scientists say it takes the subconscious mind that long to accept a new behavioral pattern.

My challenge to you is to settle on a routine that works for you. Then, follow through with it consistently for at least three weeks. At the end of that time, your strategy will be set in stone. With a little flexibility and a lot of patience, you'll see how easy it can be to accomplish your goals.

20| MIRROR, MIRROR ON THE WALL . . . YOU KNOW WHO'S HOLDING YOU BACK (PART 2)

With a little flexibility and a lot of patience,
you'll see how easy it can be to accomplish your goals.

In the last section, I started with the question "Who's holding you back?" None of us need to look any further than the closest mirror. The answer to the question, of course, is you. Each of us possesses the unique ability to make the right choices to produce alignment and achieve peak performance in everything we do.

One of the foundational qualities found in the lives of most successful people is the ability to apply consistent strategies and totally commit to self-improvement. This is the key to achieving any goal—whether you're trying to diet or succeed in business.

In part one on this topic, I gave you five tips that will help you apply consistent strategies. I would like to give you a few more to consider:

- **Apply the yin and yang to your efforts.** Yin and yang is an ancient Taoist concept that says all things exist in a harmonious paradox.

- **Be patient in your quest.** Remember, Rome wasn't built in a day.

- **Patience is a skill; practice it and you will get better at it.** Whether it means delaying gratification long enough to put in the grunt work or waiting twenty-four hours before sending off a complaint letter, the practice of patience benefits everyone.

- **Balance your actions with passive patience.** Learn to achieve the balance between being active and passive, and watch your consistent strategies pay off—BIG!

Remember, it takes twenty-one days, on the average, to change a habit. So, practice, practice, practice until it becomes your reality.

My challenge to you is to settle on a routine that works for you. Then, follow through with it consistently for at least three weeks. With a little flexibility and a lot of patience, you'll see how easy it can be to accomplish your goals.

21 | BUSTING PATTERNS WITH "PIVOTING"

If the vision you have for yourself in the future does not have an emotional buzz, your efforts will be futile.

"But I can't stay on track."

"I keep falling back into the same rut."

What can you do? Use a pattern buster . . .

Negative patterns, habits, and ways of thinking do not go away easily. Ask any smoker, alcoholic, or power junkie. It's hard to eliminate bad habits.

Earlier in this book we pinpointed that C.A.S. (consistently applied strategies) coupled with using a gold dot (a trigger for your emotional buzz-dominant thought) would take you further and faster.

Yet, getting out of the rut remains difficult . . .

For those of you who have read *The Ant and the Elephant,* you may remember Action Step #4:

> Institute pattern busters. Once you recognize yourself or your team playing out the pattern of negativity, interrupt this thought by saying, "Thank you, but that is not part of my vision. My vision is . . ." Experience the vision in detail.

Note: If the vision you have for yourself in the future does not have an emotional buzz attached, your efforts will be futile. This vision qualifies as an emotional buzz only if creating, building, or being part of something elicits an exciting physical reaction in your body.

By having your conscious mind (the ant) converse with the massive subconscious mind (the elephant) you can bust *any* pattern. It is called "pivoting" and here's how it works . . .

The second you notice a negative thought or behavior that is *not* aligned with your emotional buzz vision say, "Thank you, but that is not part of my vision. My vision is (insert your emotional buzz, gold dot, vision statement here)." Interrupt this negative thought or behavior until it eventually stops showing up. In the place of the negative pattern, you have a positive pattern that, over time, becomes a new habit.

Do this, and the pattern buster has worked for you too.

22 | SEEK THE DISCOMFORT

Seek the discomfort and you will grow, learn, and prosper.

Think of the most profound lessons you've learned in your life.

Were you comfortable or uncomfortable?

Uncomfortable!

Hence the path to your goals *must* include discomfort if you have any desire to reach your goals. Yet seeking pleasure is a far more instinctive response than seeking pain.

Seeking discomfort is not about

- masochism. (For some that is pleasure . . . I don't get that and we just won't go there)

- finding a new victim story. (Tell a story of woe more than once and you're a victim candidate)

- doing damage to yourself or others. (yada, yada, yada)

Seeking discomfort is about:

- courage to endure some degree of awkwardness.

- a willingness to get in over your head (but not too far).

- a curiosity about the unknown.

Seek the discomfort and you will grow, learn, and prosper. (To boldly go . . .)

23| **YARD YOGA**

Yard work will do wonders.

Exercise.

The word alone can give some of us the guilty hives.

There's the thought of getting up early, glancing in the mirror and realizing that your head looks like the outline of Africa, stumbling to the gym, hoping to get the treadmill that is not under the look-at-me-and-my-jiggly-bits-spotlight . . . ugh. I think I'll just sleep in.

Well, there is a gratifying way to exercise and look like a Survivor finalist all at once.

Yard yoga.

Get up with the sun and put your yard work clothes on and walk straight past the automatic, electricity-burning, gas-guzzling machinery. Bring out the hand tools and do your ticker some good.

Do some digging. Aerate the lawn. Edge along the driveway. Clip the shrubs. Water the plants with a watering can instead of a hose. Weed, prune, saw, carry. Just keep moving and active in peace and quiet (sans iPod).

Should you live in an apartment, there are elderly neighbors who could use a hand. (Here's a tip . . . let them know before you shape the hedge into the Arc de Triomphe.)

Yard Yoga will do wonders for your body, your psyche, your relationship with Mother Nature and your personal space.

Oh, and when it's winter and there's snow everywhere—that shovel's calling your name.

24| **HUMBLE GENIUSES**

*Combine authenticity with your empathy for
others and you have found the genius of being humble.*

"What the world needs is geniuses with humility.
There are so few of us left."

—*Oscar Levant*

Don't you love that quote? There is a grain of truth in this comedic phrase. Let's dive in and see what that is:

Be humble. It is not "do humble," it is "BE HUMBLE." Being humble is not an act. There are people who can act humble but once you get to know them, they are anything but. Some have been acting humble for so long that they themselves don't even know it's an act.

Lose your agenda. Being humble is about losing your agenda. You can set your own agenda aside with a combination of empathy and authenticity.

Nurture empathy. Empathy is one of the first human personality traits that infants exhibit. Years ago, our one-year-old toddler Isabella took her mother by the hand over to a crying baby to help the upset infant feel better. Empathy is instinctual. Empathy gets lost when people have an agenda that overrides everything else.

Show true authenticity. Authenticity is about showing who you truly are. Salespeople, politicians, blind daters, and anyone else with a vested interest in "closing the deal" may hide their authenticity because of fear of being rejected. But by doing this, they actually put the deal in jeopardy.

"But I hid all the bad stuff and showed only the good stuff. Why would the sale be compromised?"

Think of someone you are closest to, most attracted to. Do you know about all his or her warts? Of course. So the people who are the most authentic are the most attractive.

Yet, salespeople, politicians, blind daters, and those other people with an agenda can get stymied and not know why.

Now, combine this authenticity with your empathy for others and you have found the genius of being humble.

25 | THE ELIXIR OF MIRTH

Find the humor and share the bliss.

There's nothing better than the sound of a child's laughter (except for the sound of your spouse saying, "You're right, honey").

With a boy and two girls (aged eight, seven, and five) our family has plenty of opportunities to laugh.

Recently I realized that running into walls and making elastic faces was losing its comedic value. To keep the audible elixir of mirth in the air, I had to get creative. I had to get more sophisticated yet silo my humor to be gender specific and age appropriate.

The moment to try out new strategies arrived as my son and I lay under the stars on a warm summer evening.

Out in nature we gazed at millions of stars. Prominently displayed in the night sky were two bright 'stars.'

"Some of the 'stars' are actually planets, Max," I said with fatherly conviction. "That bright one on the left is Venus. That other bright one up and to the right is Mars. And you can even see Uranus but it helps if you have a mirror."

The tranquility of the moment was immediately transformed into belly-busting laughter from my eight-year-old son. He guffawed until his stomach hurt.

A moment of joy that lasted for days. (Without slapstick bruises or face cramps for me to endure.)

Find the humor and share the bliss. (Unless you're an accountant. Then rub a calculator all over your body while saying "I love you Number Bunny.")

Ah . . . enough sage wisdom for you, our cherished reader.

My next challenge? Hearing the sweet sound of "You're right, honey."

(A man can dream, can't he?)

26| YOU'RE FUNNIER THAN YOU THINK

Humoring yourself can add years to your life.

Can you laugh at yourself or do you let others do it for you?

Humoring yourself can add years to your life, add a spring to your step, replace high-fiber meals, and make your second cousins better looking.

A few years back, my wife Michelle and I took all our employees out to an improv theater. Throughout the evening the comedy troupe asked the audience for ideas.

Halfway through the show they asked the patrons for a word that starts with R.

Immediately, evidently allowing her neurons to take a detour, my wife yelled out "orchestra."

There was a long, dumbfounded pause, followed by my wife bursting out in laughter with the entire room in close pursuit.

We still laugh about that comical moment, although I tend to be the one bringing it up more than my wife.

Come to think of it . . . she often brings up the time when we were dancing a few years back. You know those people who *think* they know how to dance, but can't?

Apparently, I am one of them-there Delusional Dancers.

After leaving me on the dance floor to fully express myself, in what I alone felt was poetry in motion, Michelle came back to the edge of the dance floor frozen in horror. I had taken my dancing to a new level. It was a combination of Krumping and a Norwegian Fisherman's Herring Two-step.

A woman standing beside Michelle asked, "Do you see that white-haired guy out there?"

"Uh huh," Michelle nodded without turning her head in fear of being guilty by association.

With a serious, compassionate look on this bystander's face, the woman asked a final question.

"Do you think he's deaf?"

We still laugh about that one too.

Humor really is a wonderful medicine, with no co-pay or insurance premiums. Learn to laugh at yourself and with others. Your stomach lining and second cousins will thank you for it.

27 | **THE WONDER OF LOOKING STUPID**

Seek the discomfort and you will have your own growth opportunity.

At the risk of looking stupid, my discomfort can be our mutual gain. Let me explain . . . At our children's school, parent involvement is the backbone of the learning infrastructure.

It started innocently enough. The school asked me to give a speech at an event. Had I stopped there, I might have been tagged as Vince The Olympian.

Next year, three dads and myself were wand-holding, tutu-wearing, Fundraising Fairies for a school supplies fund. Saying yes turned into the four of us in "ballet glory" in front of the entire parent assembly.

Olympics, schmo-lympics. Call me Tutu Dad.

It probably didn't help that for a Halloween function with Cheap Trick performing, my wife and I went as ladies of the night. Michelle was "A Cheap Trick." I was "An Even Cheaper Trick." Suffering through high heels, fake eyelashes, and a sequined dress from hell was nothing compared to the emotional scars I must have inflicted on my kids. "Why's Daddy wearing a dress?" was heard as we walked out the door. (I am not sure how the babysitter handled that one.)

Ballet Bozo? Oh, no. Now it's Natasha, Lady of the Night.

Recently, at a Hollywood-themed school fundraiser a few of us decided to do a group dress up. Our five wives went as Marilyn Monroe. The guys went as one of the Rat Pack. With my pale skin and white hair, I was a shoo-in as Sammy Davis Jr. Two and a half hours of makeup and black hair paint later, I became the Candy Man. Actually, that was fun!

Bye-bye, Natasha . . . Hello Mr. Bojangles.

Last week, the school called with a request. Would a few parents consider being actors in a murder mystery at the Annual Fund Campaign dinner? Never having acted before, I thought it seemed like a challenge worth taking. Another "growth opportunity." With only one read-through and rehearsal we stepped up for our debut. We gave it our best effort but we still stunk. People got so bored of our performance they went back to their cocktail conversations. It was agony in many ways.

What on earth do people think now?

What does it matter what they think?

It is worrisome to think how many people are paralyzed by fear of looking stupid. (And rightfully so I guess, since I just gave you a few vivid examples of how stupid you could look.)

Yet, new funds were raised for our children's learning experience, and I gained a huge respect for any female that wears torturous heels and makeup, bonded with friends, and learned that most actors are grossly underpaid for a job they make look so easy.

By stretching I managed to play a small part in making the world a better place, grew closer to others, and learned along the way.

Contribute, connect, and grow . . . isn't that what life is all about?

What about your life? Think of the most significant contribution, connection, or growth that you've experienced. Were you comfortable or uncomfortable?

Seek the discomfort and you will then have your own growth opportunity.

You do run the risk of looking stupid. But I wonder . . .who cares?

28| WHAT WOULD STEVEN DO?

Innovation comes from the people who are spontaneous.

My brother Steven asked me the other day, "Why don't you ever write about me?" Here you go . . .

Find ways to be spontaneous. Work and play will be even more fun.

Think of the best parties you have been to. Was it a party planned in advance, like any New Year's Eve party you've been to? Or was it something that just happened spontaneously? By springing spontaneous activities on your employees or work routine you will add more fun on the job.

My brother Steven is one of the most spontaneous people I know. Fun should be his middle name. But there is a significant twist. Rules to Steve are more guidelines than regulations. Given his spontaneous nature, this combines for a list of fun, odd, and entertaining moments.

A few weeks back, while passing the NASCAR race track, Steve took a turn towards the security gate. With dark glasses and a straight face Steve indicated that he was expected in the infield. As he was finishing his 120-mile-per-hour first lap in his rental car, security caught up and escorted him out.

A few months back, Steve asked the TSA security official at the airport if anybody had ever been passed through the X-ray machine. She said no. Without much thought (obviously), Steve lay down and was passed through the machine. Steve was traveling alone.

A few years back, a bunch of friends were on the dance floor. Out of the corner of my eye I saw Steve bolt across the dance floor and dive out the window. Seconds later he climbed back in the building and kept dancing.

A few decades back, on a date with his girlfriend, Steve pulled up to the ticket booth at an outdoor drive-in theatre. Seconds before they pulled up to the window, Steve turned to his date and said, "Stare straight ahead and don't say a word." This was followed by Steven saying to the ticket taker, "Would I have to pay if my girlfriend was deaf and blind?" With a dumbfounded look on the attendant's face, Steve paid for one and drove in.

Every organization or family should have a Steve in its midst . . . someone to be spontaneous and fun. A former CEO and president of SC Johnson and Nike said, "One of my jobs is to protect the crazies." He knew that innovation came from the people who were spontaneous.

Say what you will about Steve's sense of judgment, he is fun to hang with, he is my brother, and I love him for who he is.

Find ways to be spontaneous. If you get stuck, ask yourself, what would Steven do? (Followed by a few more questions about the law, your own safety, getting other people into trouble, etc.)

29 | **HOW TO BE COOL**

You are cool when you are yourself.

Here's a story about the student becoming the teacher.

"Why do people smoke if they know it's bad for them?" asked my eight-year-old son, Max.

"I guess they start smoking because they want to be cool and then they can't quit," I answered.

Max was silent. I immediately took this as a teaching opportunity.

"People are cool when they score a goal in soccer or work hard in school . . ." I said before Max cut me off.

"No, Dad, you are cool when you are yourself."

It was my turn to be silent. Max was right! Finally I asked, "Where did you learn that, Max?"

"Why do people always ask me that?" he replied. "I just know. That's all."

"Sorry, Max. You just taught me another lesson. Thanks." Then I shut my mouth. Zipped lips are best when a student is learning from his eight-year-old teacher.

30| HOW DO YOU WANT TO BE REMEMBERED?

Wouldn't you want to go doing something you love, smack in the middle of a dozen projects, with a smile on your face?

Prepping for an '80s theme party, dressed like Richard Simmons, I had an interesting thought . . .

What if I had a heart attack right then and there?

Picture it: with electric blue nylon shorts, a tie-dye singlet, white aerobic shoes, and a curly-haired wig, being wheeled into the emergency room. What would the ER medical staff think?

Then I had another thought . . .

How would my story compare to a forty-four-year-old wheeled in, wearing Chinos and a golf shirt?

Story one: Guy dies wearing free golf shirt.

or

Story two: Guy kicks the bucket wearing a singlet with a pink heart in the middle of it.

Think of the ramifications. On one hand they'd say, "Did you hear about Bob? He had a heart attack and he died at forty-four."

On the other hand, they could be saying, "Did you hear about Vince? He died wearing a Richard Simmons outfit with sparkles on his arms and legs."

The question isn't about the ideal way you want to pass on. The question is: What story do you want told when your time is up?

The bigger question is: Does the story involve how you were living life or is there a story at all?

There is a new book by Nando Parrado called *Miracle in the Andes*. It is an amazing recollection of his seventy-two-day ordeal of surviving a plane crash in the Andes and eventually hiking out against all odds. One segment of the story is how he returned home, where his father and the rest of his inner circle carried on without him. Parrado was struck by the interesting perspective of passing away and months later seeing what affect it had on the world in general.

Allow me to paraphrase: "Without me in the world, everything seemed to go on as it was. I realized how insignificant my life was."

Since his ordeal, Parrado has raced cars, married the woman of his dreams, raised two wonderful daughters, and now runs five companies and stays in close contact with his friends and family. This dude has a story.

Parrado never planned on being in a plane crash and I don't plan on having a heart attack dressed up as an effeminate aerobics icon. But it does make sense to live life to the fullest, because you never know when you will be wheeled into the ER with a code blue.

It's okay to want to die in your sleep . . . but think that one over.

Wouldn't you want to go doing something you love, smack in the middle of a dozen projects with a smile on your face?

What story do you want people to tell?

How do you want to be remembered?

C'mon people. You can do it! And one, two, three, feel it? Yeah you do!

31 | WHERE ARE YOU FROM?

Being in the moment is paramount.

Ask Yossi Ghinsberg where he is from and his answer, at first, sounds glib . . .

"From right here."

Yet Ghinsberg is anything but glib. The seeds of this answer can be traced back to his captivating story of survival in the wilds of the Amazon jungle. During an adventure with three friends, tragedy struck and only two in the group returned. Ghinsberg's harrowing experience taught him a great deal about the nature of life (*Jungle*, Boomerang New Media, 2005).

There are three insights you can gain from Ghinsberg's answer to "Where are you from?"

Insight #1: Where you are from can be a state of mind instead of a physical position. What a gift of freedom you give your psyche if you are not defined by place or city.

Insight #2: Being in the moment is paramount. What a gift of enlightenment you give yourself if you truly live in the here and now.

Insight #3: You are 100 percent present with the person asking the question. What a gift of attention you give the person you are with.

The next time someone asks where you are from, sincerely answer, "From right here."

What a wonderful gift you give!

32 | GOOD NEWS, YOU'RE IN A MESS

For those of you who are struggling right now and are in a mess, this is good news. You are halfway there.

There is only one right way to clean a closet.

1. Empty it and surround yourself in a mess.
2. Keep what you want or need and discard the rest.

Your mind is like a closet. You can stuff personal issues inside and shut the door. You can deal with issues now and then, but the closet never gets organized. Or, you can empty out the darn thing and decide what you want or need to keep and discard the rest.

For those of you who are struggling right now and are in a mess, this is good news. You are halfway there. For those of you with no issues to deal with . . .

What does your closet look like?

33 | BACKSTROKE IN A PETRI DISH

If you have problems in your relationships at home or at work, then you likely have your own issues to deal with.

The best time to leave a relationship is when it is working well.

The worst time to leave a job is when things are going wrong.

Face it. If you have problems in your relationships at home or at work, then you likely have your own issues to deal with. The issues you have must be addressed now so that you don't drag them to your next relationship or job.

So, don't leave yet.

To manage tough times and difficult personal issues, treat your situation the way a scientist would analyze a petri dish experiment. As you know, the petri dish is a controlled environment where conclusions can be drawn from a given experiment.

Here are three things to do with your new experiment:

Get an outside perspective. Counseling or executive coaching from an objective third party will act like the scientist looking in the petri dish. An outside perspective can be priceless. Remember there are good scientists and poor ones. Find a good one through referrals and personal interviews.

Objectify your perspective. Leverage learning tools like books, CDs and online resources. As you attempt to sort out your issues (which are most likely subconscious) an objective perspective will help you analyze your own petri dish.

Do the backstroke in your petri dish. Pushing for answers about your own life is as logical as trying to make a flower grow faster by pulling it out of the ground. Actively lounge in your petri dish as if it were an experiment in the art of allowing.

Now that you have uncovered the issues at hand, you have a better, more objective handle on whether the relationship or responsibility is really worth leaving.

Keep doing the backstroke in your petri dish. It will help you breathe easier, and you'll still cover a good deal of distance.

34 | A LIFE OR DEATH PERSPECTIVE

Turn your opinions into questions.

Never underestimate the power of an outside perspective . . .

The Texas sun was relentless the day John and his brother decided to visit the police impound lot. A few days earlier this same sun was responsible for the brutal demise of their father, who had been randomly carjacked and forced into the trunk of his own car.

Standing before the open trunk, in the vicious, still heat, John said he wanted to get in and understand what their father must have endured in his last moments.

After John's eyes adjusted, he immediately noticed how his dad tried to pry open the lid with a crowbar. He tracked the next step to the broken taillight where he imagined his dad attempting to press the outside button to let himself out.

As John attempted to reach the trunk button, his brother suddenly said, "A little higher, now inside and towards your wrist."

Enlightened with an external point of view, John popped the trunk.

The Texas sunshine flooded the trunk. John clearly saw the immense value of an outside perspective. A perspective that would have saved his father's life!

What is the outside perspective that you can learn from?

Here are three things that you can do to leverage perspectives around you:

Let go. Instead of trying to be right all the time. Turn your opinions into questions. In a conversation that you have later today, catch yourself being determined to be right. Stop! Take a breath. Now start asking questions without any agenda towards a specific answer. Do not lead the conversation to confirming what you know. Look for things that you don't know. Let go of being right.

Let in. An outside perspective must *never* be underestimated. A pharmaceutical executive once mentioned to me that I had never sold pharmaceuticals and dismissed the services that I was offering. "That is exactly why you need me," I replied. "The only opinions you are receiving so far are from people on the inside. Answers from the outside can be quick, concise, and clear." (Can you say six-figure contract?) Let in an outside perspective.

Let out. When clothes get tight we let out some seams here and there. Your brain can work the same way. Our elephantine subconscious minds are determined to have a tight grip on beliefs, attitudes, and truths. Changing the subconscious elephant may be difficult but letting out the seams or expanding our beliefs may just be what we need to breathe easier. For example, when the speaking market shrunk by over 30 percent in 2000, my company saw a $4 billion industry plummet below $3 billion. We immediately sought an outside perspective. A perspective from someone who had been in the business longer than us, from someone who had thrived during a downturn in the '80s. Her advice? Instead of looking at the 30 percent drop in business, focus on the $3 billion pie waiting to be sliced up. We decided to target our piece of that pie. With an outside perspective, what seemed to be a restrictive situation was eased by letting out the proverbial seams on what seemed to be true.

35 | WHO'S ON YOUR BOARD?

*To make important decisions, you solicit ideas
from your personal board of directors.*

You are the chairman of YOU Incorporated. To make important decisions, you solicit the ideas from your board of directors. Who is on your board?

Try the technique used by Peter Thomas before he became the übersuccessful entrepreneur that he is today.

According to Thomas, when he started his business he couldn't afford to have a real board of directors. So, he made one up. Thomas put pictures of notable people facing his desk, like a dream team of amazing thinkers. He read the biographies of each of these people. Thomas learned what made these world leaders and experts tick and how they thought.

Imagine . . . Peter Thomas would get to a critical decision and then he would scan the photos. He would look at a picture of JFK and wonder what he would do. He would look at a photo of Gandhi and wonder what he would say. He would scan to a photo of Einstein and imagine how he would tackle a problem. He would look over to a picture of Mother Theresa and visualize how she would act.

Who would you put on your board of directors?

36| LONDON'S 2012 OLYMPICS—WHAT DOES IT MEAN TO YOU?

International understanding. Fair play. Striving for excellence.

IOC president Jacques Rogge opened a sealed envelope and declared: "The International Olympic Committee has the honor of announcing that the Games of the 30th Olympiad in 2012 are awarded to the city of London."

Thousands watching a live feed from Singapore launched into a roar of cheers, screams, and applause as London was announced. Paris, Madrid, New York, and Moscow had poured their hearts and souls into securing the 2012 Olympics as well. But, for a second time since 1948, London will host the world.

What makes the Olympic Games such an important event worldwide? What is the gravitational pull that brings people from five continents together? Why are the Olympics more popular today than ever before? What do the Olympic Games mean to you?

There are three guiding principles followed by the International Olympic Committee. These principles are the foundation of sport and competition. They are so pure of intent that they are impossible to refute but a daily struggle to uphold.

- **International understanding.** Our global economy is an interconnected network of cultures brought together. The Olympics represent this in a forum of sport.

- **Fair play.** Competition, in its purest form, is a person or team competing fairly and honestly. The Olympics sends a message to everyone: Be honest, be fair, play by the rules, be ethical.

- **Striving for excellence.** The motto of the Olympic Games is *Citius, Altius, Fortius.* Swifter, Higher, Stronger. Not swiftest, highest, strongest. It is *not* about being the best (despite all the media attention on medal counts). It is about striving for personal excellence.

Between now and 2012 London hopes that the Olympic flame has been sparked for all to remember to strive for excellence, play fair, and live in a world of international understanding.

37| NO FATE WORSE THAN FOURTH

In the Olympics, you don't lose. You win second place . . .
you win third place . . . you win fourth place.

Pitiful is the look in an athlete's eyes who just placed fourth at the Olympics.

Laurent Sistach placed fourth in the 1992 Olympic Winter Games in Speed Skiing. I found him in the bar the night following the finals. Hiding behind a glass of Jagermeister, he looked up slowly, shrugged, and gazed back in the glass as if it were a crystal ball showing his future.

For eight years he had trained hard. His reward? He got to watch the medal ceremony wondering why those ancient Greeks didn't have a fourth podium, an aluminum medal, and a token crown of olive branches.

Somebody has got to lose, though. (Besides, imagine being a fourth-place luger. Or a fourth-place doubles luger . . .)

At the Olympics there really are only a few dozen really happy athletes. The rest are thinking about a small mistake, equipment failure, or a crappy seed.

The great equalizer is something that nobody knows about, though. It is the athletes' party at the end.

If you watched the closing ceremonies of the twentieth Olympic Winter Games, realize that fifty-plus buses lined up outside Stadio Olympico in Turino waiting to take the athletes off to a party that was only for them.

No coaches, no officials, no media . . . just music, dancing, and, for many, the prospect of getting wasted.

Figure skaters run around like Lilliputians between the legs of lumbering bobsledders. Lubricated skiers mix with semi-vertical lugers. Gunless biathletes with toothless hockey players. Spry ski jumpers with red-eyed boarders. Medalists with nonmedalists. But every single Olympian has the same thing on his or her mind. *It's over and I am free for this one night.*

Even the person who placed fourth is free.

The Greeks have a saying that the fourth-place athlete should remember in the days and weeks following. In the Olympics, you don't lose. You win second place . . . you win third place . . . you win fourth place.

Ah . . . bugger it. You placed fourth and the feeling sucks.

Cheers Laurent! Wherever you are.

38 | A FANTASTIC AMOUNT OF MONEY

Anytime you refer to money, use the word "fantastic."
Your subconscious will be encouraged to move in a
financially abundant direction.

"Richard Branson is stinking rich."

"Donald Trump has an ungodly amount of money."

"The guys who own Google are filthy rich."

Don't talk about money like that!

If money is something that has been eluding you lately, the reason might be on the tip of your tongue.

As you know from *The Ant and the Elephant,* if the activity ratio between the conscious and subconscious mind is equivalent to the ratio between an ant and an elephant . . . it's the elephantine subconscious mind you want to engage.

If you use words like stinking, ungodly, and filthy when referring to money, then you are training the elephant to walk in the exact opposite direction from money.

The solution is simple . . . Any time you refer to money, use the word "fantastic." The elephant, your subconscious, will be encouraged to move in a financially abundant direction.

Did you know that Branson, Trump, and those Google guys have a fantastic amount of money?

39 | THE ILLUSION OF MONEY

Keep thinking what you want to create.

Money is really only a thought.

In a conversation with my friend George the other day he brought up an interesting notion. Thousands of years ago, the currency was wheat, rice, poultry, and pigs. Since those were difficult to carry in Gucci satchels, somebody figured that gold was better.

Then the gold got too heavy to carry around so somebody stood up at a meeting and said, "Paper will now replace gold."

Then money got tight and somebody went to the guy who runs the color photocopier and said, "Print more money."

But there was more money printed than really existed. This might explain why the market crashed in 1929, because everyone wanted the money that they thought they owned but really didn't.

Somewhere along the line, checks became fun for a while. Then paper money seemed so nineteenth century and the people who figured there was a future in plastic created credit cards.

Then the computer people, not to be outdone, created digital money and online banking.

Still, money that you *think* is there is not really there. Wherever "there" is.

So money is just a thought. And a thought is just energy between synapses in your brain. So then money is just a collective conscious notion.

Descartes said, "I think, therefore I am." (Which is debatable because at age twelve I would have been a northerly part of the female anatomy. But I digress.)

So if you think you have money you have it (but don't really have it). If you think you have money, but you don't have it, then you are leading a manifestation of money where you will have it but not really have it.

"I think, therefore I am confused."

There, now that we solved that little issue . . . keep thinking what you want to create, but not too much or you'll think yourself into confusion.

40 | POST-IT NOTES VS. DIAMONDS

The little things matter as much as the big things.

If you are a woman, stop reading this. It's not for you.

If you are a man, I've got a tip that will save you a ton of money.

A few birthdays ago I gave my wife an expensive diamond necklace. She gushed, she swooned, she was oh-so-happy.

A couple of months later I left her a few Post-it notes laying here and there around the house. On each one, I wrote a loving note. She gushed, she swooned, she was oh-so-happy. In fact, it was *exactly* the same gushing, swooning, oh-so-happiness that I experienced a couple of months prior.

I tried the Post-it note approach a few weeks later. More gushing, swooning, oh-so-happiness.

If you want to get the "He really does care about me," message across . . . try any or all of these three ideas:

1. **Post-it notes in random places.** Point out the things that she does that you appreciate and say it how great she makes you feel.

2. **Write a letter to her parents.** Tell them how much you appreciate her and all that she contributes to your life.

3. **Write a note on a poster board but use candy bars for key words.** For example, I may be from MARS but you are the CHERRY BOMB. My heart goes TIC TAC . . . (you get the idea).

And, to all the women who ignored the directions above . . . you know what we like . . .

Food.

Did I miss anything?

41 | FIXING THE PEST PROBLEM

Let's be part of the manners revolution.

Please. Excuse me. Sorry. Thank you.

PEST for short.

What a nuisance good manners have become. This must be why people are rebelling.

Walk around most public places today and watch PEST vanishing before your very eyes. And none too soon. Why be courteous when being uncivil is so much more commonplace?

Think of a day when PEST is a nostalgic notion. Out with the old . . . in with the new. Ah, it makes the heart turn to stone just thinking about it.

Alas, sarcasm is known as the lowest form of wit. And it is time for me to make a point.

Please, excuse me, sorry, and *thank you* are words heard less today than ever. And let's not get in the blame game. Every parent that I know is nothing short of maniacal about their children's manners. Anyone reading this could easily identify with the decay of manners around us.

The question is, what do we do to correct the PEST problem?

1. **Be a PEST ambassador.** The best way to influence change and turn the tides of any situation is to lead by example. Be the kind of person who always says *please, excuse me, sorry,* and *thank you,* whenever possible. Go out of your way to say it.

2. **Exaggerate to elevate.** In 1985 I attended a two-week symposium on the Olympic movement. In attendance were militant feminists determined to get their point of gender equity across. In fact, it became annoying, since I thought they were preaching to the choir. I quizzed one of the women in a private conversation. "Why are you all being so aggressive with your cause at the conference?" Her response was something I never forgot. "Any cause worth having has to exaggerate to elevate its place in the world." So, from bra burning to a manners revolution, it's you and me who will need to exaggerate to elevate manners back where they belong. A powerful start is to make sincere eye contact when you say *please, excuse me, sorry,* and *thank you.* When appropriate, reach out and touch a forearm at the same time.

3. **Skinnerize it.** B.F. Skinner made the concept of stimulus–response famous. A certain stimulus will eventually get a predictable response. Let's encourage and reward all the PEST

behavior around us. A simple *thank you* for saying *please, excuse me,* or *sorry* will do wonders (remember the eye contact).

Now you have come to an awkward decision. Do you send this message to friends? What message does that send? Hey you mannerless churl, read this!

No, the spirit of the message is to set the wheels in motion for a new form of PEST control. Let's be part of the manners revolution.

Be a PEST ambassador to elevate the respect we all need to give and deserve to receive.

42 | THE HARDEST WORD TO SAY

When the time is right, just pucker up and say, "I'm sorry."

Why is sorry such a hard word to say?

For some people, it is a near-impossible word to utter. There are guys who would rather you pull out their eyeteeth with salad tongs before making them say sorry. What gives, people?

There are actually three "what gives":

1. I happen to believe, on no authority whatsoever, that *sorry*, when broken down, means: *sor* as in "sore" or "pain," and *ry* as in "re" or "do again." So we can plainly see that sorry means "it really pains me to do this again." People shy away from pain, and voilà, we have "what gives" number one.

2. People love to be right. Even when they are wrong they want to be right. Saying sorry is admitting wrongness. Men

especially dislike saying "sorry," mostly because they would be saying it all the time. Women also dislike saying "sorry," because they are used to being (and often are) right.

3. *Sorry*, falsely so, is perceived by the purveyor of sorryness to be a sign of weakness. *If I say sorry then I am nothing more than a wet piece of Kleenex™*, thinks the dude who won't admit he is wrong.

Alas, we come to the "what to do?" part. Saying sorry is easier if you can apply one of these three concepts:

1. **Attach a reward to it.** Recently the CEO of a $700 million software company found out that a prospect was cheesed off about an aggressive salesperson trying to push a deal too hard, too fast. A different salesperson (a woman) was assigned to the case. She said, "I think if we said sorry we could resurrect this (multimillion-dollar) deal." The CEO called up and admitted he was sorry for what had happened. The deal closed, everyone was happy.

2. **Remind yourself of the sage question: Is it more important to be right or happy?** Not a tough choice really. My wife and I had an agreement to never go to bed angry. Months later, I dismissed this agreement because I knew I was right and she was wrong. I went to bed angry. The next day, with only a couple of hours sleep, I was challenged by a friend, "So you'd rather be right than happy." Ouch. Now, I pick happy over right, any day.

3. **Get over yourself.** Is it really that bad to admit that you are sorry? Who cares if you messed up? It's human nature to make mistakes. Or, maybe you are acting like a wet piece of

Kleenex™ and it's time to face the facts. In the words of a friend and colleague, "Some people are so far up themselves, it's dark." (If I just offended you, I'm s . . . I'm s . . . I'm . . . sorry.)

Elton John even wrote a song, "Sorry Seems to Be The Hardest Word." Well, it's not so bad folks. When the time is right, just pucker up and say, "I'm sorry."

43 | **KEEP YOUR NOSE CLEAN**

Keep your nose clean and you have nothing to worry about.

You might as well not have any secrets. It's easier that way.

I should know. I talk in my sleep every night.

Which is why I have learned not to keep any secrets from my wife. Something I learned early on.

When my wife and I first knew each other, in a biblical way— after we were married of course . . . um . . . well, let's not get bogged down in details. Just picture my wife being awakened in the middle of the night to the sound of me laughing.

As she cleared her mind, she heard me say, "Trust me, I'm a gynecologist."

God knows what I was dreaming about but I have learned to keep my proverbial nose clean. Not only is it the right thing to do, but my REM verbalizations would surely cough up any wayward behavior.

Keep your nose clean and you have nothing to worry about.

44 | STOP DIGGING

When in doubt, don't.

"When you realize you're digging a hole for yourself, put the shovel down."

Advice from my mom that I probably should have remembered when I was giving a toast at a friend's wedding. I still cringe when I think about it. In fact, my wife tried to *shush* me, but what guy likes to be *shush*ed?

Anne was marrying Will in a picturesque part of the country. (The real names and details have been withheld to protect the new-lyweds and avoid any chance of making the same mistake twice.)

At the reception, I thought, *Since I am a professional speaker and all, I should probably say a few words.* As I started telling a particular story, my wife turned white. The new bride's complexion matched her dress. I got a telltale headshake and a *shush*.

Thinking I could navigate the story adeptly, I forged ahead.

Within seconds I was in a deep hole, and I was only digging deeper. Soon it was too late, and I looked like a stunt double from *Dumb and Dumber*. Later, guests pulled Will aside and said, "I thought he was a professional speaker . . ." Like any real man facing up to his mistakes, I hid in the boathouse for the next four hours.

What did I learn that I can pass on? (How about advice from my mom that I remembered all too late?)

1. **When in doubt, don't.** If you have that internal voice that says, *This probably isn't a good idea*, then hold off and think

on it for a while. If the voice is your wife, then shut your pie hole.

2. **Don't get too big for your britches.** If your ego is bigger than your reason, you are bound for a fall. Stay humble and get bigger pants.

3. **Stop digging.** It's never too late to stop and admit that you might be making a mistake. If you don't like that idea, fake a seizure and really freak 'em out.

Thanks for the advice, Mom . . . looks like I had to learn the hard way.

45 | IT'S ABOUT TIME

When you give the gift of time, it shows love and respect.

Being the son of an Olympian provides many learning opportunities. But most of the learning is by the dad, it seems.

This Quick Wit is about the quality of time between son and father, child and parent, or loved one and loved one.

Dr. Matthew Housson is a child psychotherapist. When counseling boys he knows that the best way to communicate is to do it in a tactile fashion. One technique he has is to toss a ball back and forth. This supports the research by author Michael Gurian, which identifies that a boy's natural tendency to move and be active must be supported and encouraged.

Knowing this, I decided to put the concept to use in a conversation that I had with my eight-year-old son, Max. Max and I were by the Rio Frio river. Its clear, slow-moving water is banked by thousands of smooth, flat rocks . . . irresistible fodder to every male, at any age.

As we were in this tactile, kinesthetic bliss I asked Max, "Am I too hard on you?"

Without looking sideways, Max flicked a rock sidearm and said, "Yes."

"Well, you know, Max, I want you to have the very best. I do this so that you can drive harder for bigger and better things. I am hard on you so that I can help you."

Max was searching the banks for another rock and said, while trying for another multiple skip, "Well, it's not working." His rock went *plop*.

I sat on the bank and put my elbows on my knees. "Max, when I push you I am trying to show how important you are to me. If was being soft on you then I might be letting you down."

"Dad," Max said, finally looking sideways, "that's not how it works." He darted over to a spot where he found the perfect skipping rock. He admired it for a bit, felt it in his left hand, then positioned his feet in the riverbank. "If you are soft then you show me how you care for me and respect me." Then he tossed the rock with a fluid follow-through.

"Good one," I said referring to both his four-skipper and his insight.

The greatest gift you can give another is the gift of your time. While you give this gift of time, it turns out being soft shows love and respect.

May your time with dear ones be full of love and respect!

46 | A PARENT'S JOB

Time flies and children are poised to leave home before we know it.

Our job as parents is to prepare our children to leave home. One method I have used may be helpful to you.

Each year, each child gets a trip with Dad. For about three days my son and each daughter pack their bags and we take off time to be together.

From the time they were each two years old, we went skiing, built sand castles on the beaches of Hawaii, toured Key West, hiked in the Rockies, rollerbladed South Beach, and explored Orlando. Anything and anywhere just to be one on one.

The benefits are many. Our children gain:

- confidence.

- a closer relationship with Dad.

- a broader awareness of the world.

- comfort in unfamiliar circumstances.

- memories to last a lifetime.

The idea is not where we go. To spend one-on-one time together is of prime importance. As working parents, we are aware that time flies and children are poised to leave home before we know it.

There are many lessons we can teach our children. A regular trip with Mom or Dad is a magical way to do this while preparing them for their eventual departure from the nest.

 **TARGET**

MORE MONEY AND RESULTS
SKINNY, RICH, AND IRRESISTIBLE

47| SKINNY, RICH, AND IRRESISTIBLE

Clarify the vision. Commit to the vision.
Consistently execute on the vision.

The sheer number of diet, financial, and relationship resources could cover the entire planet in a blanket of books.

Yet how can this much information fall short of creating any sustainable change in eating, spending, or communication behaviors?

Being skinnier, richer, or more irresistible in our own lives is a possibility that is often left unresolved. A person can be left scratching his or her head, asking, "What to do?"

The answer is at your fingertips . . . assuming you're still scratching your head.

Research from a study by Lee Pulos, PhD, revealed that in one second of time, your conscious mind uses two thousand neurons. Amazingly, in that same second, the subconscious mind utilizes 4 billion neurons. 4,000,000,000 neurons! Now, who's in control, your conscious mind or subconscious mind?

You can try to execute on a strategy. You attempt to appeal to your own logic. You even have little reminders (and books) around the house about healthy living, finances, or relationships. Then, a few weeks later . . . little or no results. Why?

Think of the ratio between an ant and an elephant. The ant is the conscious mind; the elephant is the subconscious mind. The ant, riding on the back of an elephant, sees only a gray, bumpy landscape.

The ant decides on a goal: Go west to the oasis. Yet, unknown to the ant, the elephant is walking east. Which way is the ant actually going? East!

People think and act the same way. People hear "it," say they get "it," and maybe they even go through the motions of executing on "it." But the results disappoint and you stand in front of the mirror going, "What am I to do?"

Here are some highlights from *The Ant and the Elephant* that you can use starting today:

Clarify the vision. Internalize a vision that creates an emotional buzz. Emotions reside deep in the elephantine subconscious. Clarify a vision that fires you up. Get the power of the elephant behind your efforts.

Commit to the vision. Commitment from an ant is not nearly as effective or powerful as a commitment from an elephant. You aren't committed until there is evidence of an emotional buy-in. There is a healthy way to commit and an unhealthy way. Just ask a lung cancer patient who is evaluating her smoking habits or a heart attack patient considering a better lifestyle. Finding a less dramatic way to change is clearly a better option.

Consistently execute on the vision. It is a fact that you will execute on your own truth and dominant thought. A fantastic tool for keeping on track is to put little gold dots all over the place. The gold dot represents your emotional buzz and acts as a reminder of your goal.

Confidence is key. Negativity destroys confidence. Keep activities and even thoughts aligned with your emotional buzz gold dot. If the infamous elephants, Nega and Holic, show up, redirect intention back on the gold dot.

Control pre-performance. Design flashcards that outline stressful scenarios. Imagine how well you would handle any given situation. Do this consistently and repeatedly. You will ultimately influence how well you perform, in almost any given situation.

48 | THE RIGHT MAN'S STUFF

Work with drive and excellence. Eliminate judgment.
Entertain the law of attraction.

Asked recently about being the first to walk on the moon, Neil Armstrong replied something along the lines of "I just happened to be next." The interviewer lauded his humble nature.

Humble maybe . . . but I'd throw in a dash of ignorance too.

Ignorance in a good way.

Neil Armstrong's answer reveals a harmless ignorance of how many people think. Read between the lines of the interviewer's question and it's as if Armstrong was singled out as lucky or he was singularly special for being the first man on the moon. Yet Armstrong doesn't see himself as lucky or special.

Where then was Neil Armstrong coming from?

Armstrong revealed himself as the kind of person who knows no other option than to drive hard toward a goal. And in that driving, excellence of execution is the minimum standard.

This mind-set helped Neil Armstrong be in the right place at the right time. In his thirty-plus years leading up to Apollo 11, Armstrong drove hard with excellent execution in his aeronautical career.

Because of his mind-set and resume, he became the first man to leave a footprint on the lunar floor.

Many readers can easily identify with Armstrong and his ignorance. You may even wonder why people don't think like you. "Why doesn't everyone drive hard with excellent execution?"

Oops . . . we just stepped on the toes of good manners and proper behavior folks. With this question we made the mistake of judging another. But Armstrong didn't make this mistake. He didn't judge other people in his "I just happened to be next" notion. His ignorance fell into a unique category. A category defined this way . . .

Ignorance without judgment is *not* naiveté. It is innocent ignorance.

There you have it. Because it is impossible to identify with a quality one has never owned, Neil Armstrong's M.O. of drive and excellence has nothing to do with coasting, being unmotivated, or living in fear. He was and is innocently ignorant of the idea of being the fortunate first man on the moon.

In the meantime, here are three things you can do to create more fortunate happenings in your life:

First, model Neil Armstrong's drive and excellence in your job. This means eliminating the natural tendency to coast, the black hole of being unmotivated, or the caustic effects of fear. The more you drive with excellence the luckier you will become.

Second, spend the rest of your life eliminating judgment from your thoughts. This is very easy advice to give, yet extraordinarily difficult to take. Personally, I made the decision to eliminate judgment from my life over ten years ago. I still struggle every day with this one. But the rewards for eliminating judgment are huge.

Eliminate judgment and you will improve your relationships, your job, and your personal life.

Third, entertain the law of attraction. Neil Armstrong attracted his opportunity to walk on the moon. With his innocent response to the interviewer's question, Armstrong exposed the law of attraction in play. His focus was more on allowing the opportunity come to him than being obsessed with being the first.

Do this, and you've got the right (wo)man's stuff in my book.

49| DOING BUSINESS WILLIE'S WAY

Customers prefer to do business with someone they like.

Phillip Van Hooser is an extraordinary thought leader in the world of leadership and customer service. (He is also a good friend!) He explains some of his ideas in his new book, *Willie's Way: 6 Secrets for Wooing, Wowing and Winning Customers and Their Loyalty.*

According to Van Hooser, "Customers have a choice when it comes to doing business—they prefer to do business with someone they like. Think how different, maybe even fun, business would be if we liked our customers and they liked us! Think how much more enjoyable the business experience would be if the bank teller greeted you by name each time or if your mechanic always returned your seat to your preferred location." The list goes on.

Here are four things I learned from Willie's Way:

1. Connecting with every customer in a memorable way is essential.

2. Have a personalized service solution for each customer's unique needs.

3. Long-lasting relationships with customers are priceless.

4. Repeat buyers recommend you to their friends!

50 | SEVEN YEARS OLD— SELLING TIPS

"No" is just a step closer to understanding where the "yes" is going to come from.

When a child gets a "no" to her question, there is a little bitty voice in her head that says, "Wrong answer, try again."

When an adult sales person hears "no," there's a far more clueless voice that says, "They don't like me."

Let's get into the mind of a seven-year-old. As chance would have it, I happen to have my own little "case study" at home. Her name is Alex and she is loath to accept the word no.

"Daddy, can I have some candy?" she asks in her sweetest voice.

"No, sorry. It's before dinner," I answer with authority.

"Please can I have a candy?"

"No."

"Can I have half?"

"No."

"Why?" she asks.

"Because it's before dinner."

"Then can I have a candy after dinner?"

"Um, well, I guess you can have half after dinner."

"Daddy," she says, as direct eye contact and her mother's hazel eyes bore a hole in my willpower, "if I can have a whole candy I will eat all my dinner."

"That's blackmail," I protest in vain.

"I don't know what blackmail is but I do know that having a nutritious meal is important for me to grow up healthy."

"Right. So, I can have a candy and a full meal. Everyone wins."

I stand there not sure how I got backed into this corner.

"Right. Thanks Daddy." Followed by a kiss and dash for the other room. As she leaves the room I spot the candy that must have been in her hand the whole time.

It is at this point I recognize a recurring thought I have been having. When child labor laws permit, I will put my daughter in charge of sales at my own company.

"Hello Ms. Meeting Planner, will you book my dad to speak at your company's next conference?"

"No, sorry . . ."

(Doesn't Ms. Planner know she doesn't stand a chance?)

As for your sales career . . . don't think "no" means they don't like you. Use Alex's technique (used by children worldwide): "No" is just a step closer to understanding where the "yes" is going to come from.*

*Green Eggs and Ham by Dr. Seuss features over two dozen objections before the furry skinny dude gets a yes. Evidently, this is a learning tool for children in their mission to break down weak-minded parents.

51| THE ABCs OF GETTING YOUR WAY

Attention. Benefit. Creativity.

Getting your way equals sales. Selling success depends on the ABCs.

A stands for *Attention.*

Get the attention of your prospect. There are examples all over the place. Franchises use consistent branding that is distinct, food and beverage companies use the aroma the second you walk in, moms around the world add the middle name when trying to grab their child's attention. (Vincent Thomas Poscente, stop whacking your brother over the head with that hockey stick!)

If you are advertising, writing or speaking, grab your audience's attention by being unconventional. If you have ever seen my Olympic keynote, I open by standing on a chair describing what it is like to travel at 135 miles per hour on skis. Vietnam POW, Charlie Plumb opens by silently pacing the exact dimensions of his prison cell. News channels put the shocking stuff up front to reel in bombarded-with-information audiences. The unwritten slogan is, "If it bleeds, it leads."

B stands for *Benefit.*

After you have your prospect's attention you'd better deliver some value. Give value and this is a benefit in the mind of your prospect. Humor can be the value in a funny commercial. New ideas in a marketing piece or practical insights in a sales pitch must offer value to the prospect. If you're not focused on value, the attention-getter in the beginning won't keep them.

Let's say you are on a first date. You got her attention by bringing flowers (I found wearing a thong and cowboy boots doesn't work). Follow up by dropping in value nuggets like the facts that you have a job and that Pinto out front is not yours.

C stands for *Creativity*.

Every step in your marketing approach must be creative or it will get lost in the plethora (a.k.a. lotsa) of stuff that hits people every day. The title, content, information, images, artwork, everything must exude creativity. A little creativity in many places adds up to a lot.

Book titles are a good example. What if John Gray had named his book *Men are Strangely Different from Women* rather than *Men are from Mars, Women are From Venus*? What if a hotelier did all the advertising and value add, then offered bland, featureless rooms? What if Muhammad Ali had never uttered a sound bite like, "I will float like a butterfly and sting like a bee"—would he have been able to sell the rights to his name/brand for $50 million?

Right now, think of something you are trying to sell. Be it a service, product, or idea, put it on a desk in front of you and carefully analyze your offering. Does your approach start with an attention-getter? Do you offer benefits to the buyer? Does everything you say, show, or deliver ooze creativity?

Remember the quote: "Nothing happens until somebody sells something." Well, your chances of selling something are severely hobbled unless you follow the ABCs of getting your way.

52| WHEN ALL ELSE FAILS, GO DEEPER, LOOK DEEPER (PART 1)

A person's results are ultimately in keeping with the truth he had in the first place.

Most leaders eventually learn, when there is a problem, to look in the mirror. In our business we learned this lesson first-hand. A few years ago, we pushed our sales, team in a direction that seemed quite logical. To increase our sales, we effectively said, "Change your actions and you will get new results." We found some modest short-term corrections, but over time, the production went right back to the same old level. We didn't know why. This problem recurred until we asked ourselves a deeper, more crucial question: What are the factors that motivate the actions producing these results?

Judgments lead to action or inaction. They are much like layers in a coconut. We get past one layer and there is another layer underneath. Sometimes, it's tough to get past the first layer or two. We asked yet another question: Where do people's judgments come from? Then, bingo, we found the root of our problem. Judgments are fed by a person's attitudes and beliefs, which make up that person's truth. A person's attitudes, opinions, and truths act as a filter.

A person will receive information and pass it through his personal filter (as the truth). He will make a judgment then take action or not. This ultimately produces results. We were amazed to find that a person's results are ultimately in keeping with the truth he had in the first place. This meant that the poor sales (the results) were produced by each individual's truth. It did not matter what actions we tried to get employees to take; our real battle was with their attitudes, opinions, and truths.

Next . . . a great strategy for achieving the desired R.E.S.U.L.T.S!

53| WHEN ALL ELSE FAILS, GO DEEPER, LOOK DEEPER (PART 2)

Repeat the vision, exchange information, and strategize consistent application.

As a company, our performance breakthrough with our sales staff did not occur until we asked ourselves a deeper, more crucial question: What are the factors that motivate the actions producing poor results?

We had finally recognized that a person's poor sales (the results) were ultimately in keeping with the truth he or she had in the first place. So, it did not matter what actions we tried to get the employees to take; our real battle was with their attitudes, opinions, and truths.

To overcome this, we successfully engaged a strategy based on the acronym R.E.S.U.L.T.S. Here are the first three parts of the strategy:

Repetition of the corporate vision. We shifted from just putting our corporate vision on the wall to getting the team tuned into what the vision meant to them. At our Monday morning meetings we revisited the vision, with people presenting on how the corporate vision would contribute to their personal vision.

Exchange information in open forums. Again, at the Monday morning meetings, we would visit last week's sales and progress. Instead of focusing on the actions towards a good sale, we had success stories where the salesperson would describe what the sale meant to him. The benefit was twofold. First, it kept the salesperson in tune with his personal attitudes around the sale, and second, other employees identified with that person's attitude and recognized it as his own.

Strategize consistent application. As an Olympic athlete I relied on a strategy that was consistently applied. Unfortunately, salespeople, as a rule, rely less on strategy and more on a "hit or miss" approach. Therefore, we sat down with each person and mapped out his or her own individual strategy for achieving desired results.

Next . . . the final four strategies for achieving the desired R.E.S.U.L.T.S!

54| WHEN ALL ELSE FAILS, GO DEEPER, LOOK DEEPER (PART 3)

Understand fears, locate core values, tie in the corporate vision, and support decisions.

Here are the final four parts of a strategy we successfully engaged based on the acronym R.E.S.U.L.T.S. that enabled our company achieve performance breakthrough with our sales staff:

Understanding unconscious fears. Mismanaged fear produces poor results and many fears are unconscious. Here is an example of how we found these fears. We asked one of our sales staff what her preferred results would be. Her first response was to make more money. More questions revealed, making more money meant more time working. After a few more questions she said she got into sales to have more freedom. It was as if a light bulb was turned on. This person realized she unconsciously thought that making more money meant less freedom. Lo and behold, it was not the market. It was her getting in her own way. She instantly made a decision to work smarter on moneymaking activities, delegate the others, and retain her freedom. When all team members' fears are outlined then they can help one another deal with and eventually overcome fear.

Locate each team member's core values. We used a series of questions that uncovered what each person was good at. Then we asked them to identify the experiences that produced positive results in their lives. Again, like peeling the coconut, we looked for core experiences. For example, one fellow was known for entertaining other people. The experience he sought was to make people laugh. Underneath that experience, the core value was making a difference in the lives of others. Now he has his ultimate objective in making a good sale. Instead of focusing on just his actions (i.e., the killer close), his approach in the sale was shifted to making a positive difference in his prospect's life.

Tie the corporate vision with the individual's core values. This was simple. Each person had to come up with three of his or her core values that paralleled or fit with the corporate vision. We instantly made each person a tangible, identifiable part or our corporate vision. Our vision became their vision and vice versa.

Support their decisions. Command and control leadership is DEAD! Our strategy was useless if we did not trust each person's decisions. We made research materials available, hired speakers, purchased sales tapes, but none of it was mandatory. The benefits were instant. The moment we stopped pushing, the salesperson stopped pushing back. He stood on his own two feet and made his own decisions. We built trust and respect by trusting and respecting each individual's decisions.

Our corporate results shifted slowly at first. We were patient and stuck to our plan. By the end of our fiscal year we had doubled production and seemed to have more fun doing so. Twelve months later we doubled sales again. Not bad for a simple shift in processes and systems.

Effectively, we lead by clarifying the organizational goals alongside the individual goals. The process design involved the team. All the while, we learned the different leadership styles of each individual. We learned the importance of clarifying our own roles, which meant we better understood our employees. We focused on R.E.S.U.L.T.S. to get great results!

55 | WHERE WILL THE MONEY COME FROM?

Engage an abundance mentality, add value, and pivot your focus.

Maharishi Mahesh Yogi was questioned at the beginning of his ambitious plans to roll out Transcendental Meditation to the world. "Where will the money come from?" he was asked. His instant response, "Wherever it is right now."

Money can pose a great deal of strain on relationships and one's sleep. Wondering where the money will come from may be a question on your mind.

Here are three things to do when you find yourself worried about money.

1. **Engage an abundance mentality.** With the abundance mentality, you will attract money. Fears surrounding money will keep you stuck. (Borrowed money must be treated with a healthy amount of respect.) Tip: keep a hundred-dollar bill in your wallet at all times.

2. **Add value.** When the money flow is flowing in the wrong direction, add value! If times are tough, step up with value in everything you do. This will eventually get the money flowing in the right direction, towards you. Tip: in the next two hours add value to a project or personal interaction.

3. **Pivot your focus.** If money is tight, chances are your focus is on the lack of money. Pivot your focus on what you do have. Money woes can be ingrained patterns of thought. These patterns can be passed on from generation to generation. Stop the madness! When you notice you are thinking about what you lack, pivot your thought onto what you have. Tip: the next time you pay your bills, interrupt the thought patterns of lack onto what you have (that hundred dollars in your wallet, for example . . .)

56| GRANNY'S SKIVVIES

If you want to perform at the highest level, have fun!

Peak performance is not just about being on your A-game. Peak performance has so much more to do with having fun!

Some friends of mine, a husband-and-wife realtor team, have a story to drive this home.

In a rush to get to a very important listing appointment, John and Libby (the real names are withheld to protect the innocent) had to dress quick to pitch a listing agreement on a multiple condo complex. The deal was worth tens of thousands of dollars. The pressure was on and they had to be on their A-game.

Libby changed into her best power suit and John flew into the laundry room to get clothes that hadn't made back to the closet yet. It was a rush, but they made it.

With seconds to spare, John and Libby pulled up to the building where their meeting would be held. Libby looked over and saw an odd grin on John's face.

"What's up? Are you ready? Why are you smiling?"

John paused and said, "You're not going to believe this. But I couldn't find my underwear in the laundry room so I had to wear your blue ones."

"Blue ones? Gross! Ahhhhh, gross . . . I don't have blue ones, those are Granny's skivvies!"

John and Libby burst out laughing. They laughed so hard, it took a couple of minutes to compose themselves.

Forty-five minutes later they had a 180-day listing contract in their hands.

The moral of the story . . . if you want to perform at the highest level, have fun! (And if all else fails, wear Granny's skivvies.)

57 | IT'S GOOD FOR BUSINESS

Have more fun at work. Be more fun at work.
Share more fun at work.

Having a quick wit at work is good for business.

To make my point . . . how about the time I was conceived?

Recently I was transferring old family eight-millimeter film to a digital format. Knowing that I was born nine months after my parents' nuptials, I was somewhat intrigued to see the telltale look on my newlywed Mom's face (for all the G rated expectations that you have, we'll call it a glow) as the film captured her walking out of the Palliser Hotel in Calgary a couple days after the wedding.

Fast-forward forty years as I checked into the renovated Palliser in Calgary and was escorted to the elevator by a sharp-dressed bellperson (-hop, -boy, -dude). With real-life, innocuous elevator music playing, I casually turned to him and said, "I think I was conceived at the Palliser Hotel."

He nodded in my direction and said, "Well . . . welcome back, sir." We both cracked up at his masterful quick wit, and the Palliser Hotel gets all sorts of PR every time I tell that story. A simple fun exchange with a bell professional was good for business.

Or how about the time when Michelle (now my wife) and I were dating and I wanted to show off my favorite Italian restaurant?

La Dolce Vita was run by Italians, staffed by Italians, and had two fun-loving Italian cooks in the kitchen. There was nothing Anglo about the place. Until I took Michelle there. After we were seated a twenty-year-old, blond-haired, blue-eyed Swedish poster boy walked up to our table and asked for our drink order.

"What's your house wine?" I asked.

"Testa di C------," he replied.

Since I speak some Italian, I paused and said, "What did you call it?"

"Testa di C------," he said more slowly.

"Do you know what you just said?" I asked.

"No. The cooks in the back taught me how to say the wine special," as the suspicion that he was being duped crossed his face. "What . . . does it mean?"

"It means d--- head," I replied as I looked at the kitchen door and saw two short, bald guys looking through the crack in the door and giggling like twelve-year-old boys.

"Well, would you like the red d--- head or the white d--- head?" the waiter said with a slight grin.

During the dinner, the waiter did a great job and we tipped him well. We had a fun evening and it was good for La Dolce Vita's business.

Have more fun at work. Be more fun at work. Share more fun at work. Use your God-given quick-witted talents.

It's good for business!

58 | **NO RESPECT**

To get respect, pivot your focus, get level, and draw boundaries.

Siskel and Ebert caught my act and gave it one finger up.

—*Rodney Dangerfield*

The late Mr. Dangerfield built a whole comedy career around one simple concept: "I don't get no respect." This week, let's see how we can get a little R-E-S-P-E-C-T.

Pivot your focus. All too often, people who complain about not getting respect are the source of the problem. Author Earl Nightingale wrote a book on this idea. *The Strangest Secret* is essentially all about people's natural tendency to gravitate towards their current dominant thought. So make your dominant thought where you intend to be.

Get level. The need for respect is one of our basic, human wants. It is amazing how much children intensely desire respect. As a parent, one great technique to meet this need is to squat down and get eye to eye with kids before something is communicated. Physically talking down to kids is convenient but sends two messages. One, "I don't respect you." Two, "Let me show you how not to respect other people." As a leader, there is no need to squat, but I trust you picked up on the "talking down" part.

Draw boundaries. People are not mind readers. They don't know what you are thinking. If you don't communicate boundaries, they will tend to take a little more and a little more. Being nice doesn't mean being a pushover. Plus, no one likes a second-story balcony without at railing (read boundary). People want boundaries and respect people who set them.

59 | LEADERS . . . BE SPECIFIC

*Be specific or you might have more of a mess
to clean up than you expected.*

Each year I take my children on a trip to one of the many locations I travel to for speaking engagements. My daughters and son have been on ski trips and to Hawaiian beaches. (When my daughters hit their teen years, I'm thinking only ski trips, where they have to bundle up in many layers of warm clothing.)

Anyway, on one particular trip, I learned how important it is for leaders (of any kind) to be specific.

One of the first trips for one of my daughters was a ski trip. She was three and it was her third time skiing. She was also well into the potty training thing. (Parents, you know that unmistakable position that the "trainee" takes when requesting a cleanup. An image burned in every parent's mind only to be erased by time and a multitude of martinis.)

When we checked into the condo, we took a tour of the one bedroom, one bathroom abode. "Now," I said to my daughter as we stood by the commode, "this is where you go kaki. Just scoot yourself up, sit down, and daddy will give you a hand when you're done." (Image flashes before eyes again like a bad car wreck. Back to the story, stay focused.)

Minutes later my daughter waddled up to me, her little button pants around her ankles but her princess underwear still around her waist.

"I'm finished," she said proudly sporting a present on the backside of her Disney underwear marketing item.

"Oh sweetie . . . oh . . . that was so good but next time, let's make sure Cinderella is out of the way when you have a job to do."

Leaders beware! Be specific or you might have more of a mess to clean up than you expected.

60 | DO OR WANT TO DO

You can do, or you can just want to do.

Our eight-year-old son Max is a wise soul. He dishes out more lessons than a Berlitz crash course. The lesson Yoda Max tossed out last week was a wake-up call for me as a parent and also as a leader at work.

Recently, I have been noticing that Max has been testing my boundaries (this should end when I expire). I asked Max to brush his teeth before bed. Minutes later I realized he was no closer to the bathroom than the last time I was with him.

"Max, I don't say things twice!" I said emphatically.

"No Dad, you don't *want* to say things twice."

Dumbfounded, I realized that he was right.

Max had caught me in my own issues with having my wishes respected as a parent (and probably as a leader). If I didn't say things twice, I would never say things twice. I don't *want* to say things twice, but I often do.

Projecting down the road, what kinds of problems would continue to occur if I didn't resolve my own desires to be respected? What kind of respect would I receive from a teenage Max if I continued to make the same request with no consequence?

Time for a reality check . . . how often do I flake out on my word at work?

It boils down to the difference between *do* vs. *want to do.*

You can *want* to pick up a pen or you can pick up the pen.

You can *want* more accountability in the workplace or you can execute on processes for accountability in the workplace.

You can *want* your child to follow through on your first request or you can be clear that there is an immediate consequence.

Max and I agreed that if I had a request that I would do three things.

1. I would be in the same room.

2. I would make eye contact.

3. We would follow through on a loss of privileges.

Clearly I have a lot to work on as a parent and a leader. Hopefully, this lesson from Yoda Max is helpful to you, too.

 TARGET

HAPPY EMPLOYEES, STRONG BUSINESS
DEAD FROGS

61 | DEAD FROGS

To adapt to your environment, identify signposts, feelings, and trends.

We live in a world of instant gratification. Frustration abounds. Unless we know what to do, our world will reach the boiling point.

Action starts with you.

I heard once that if you take a frog and put it in hot water, it will immediately jump out. But put a frog in cold water and gradually turn up the heat, and it will slowly cook to death.

The point of this gruesome example: In an environment of gradual change, an organism won't know to take control before it is too late.

People in abusive relationships may find themselves caught in a caustic situation that seems impossible to leave. The Holocaust was a progressive series of events where, for millions, it became too late to escape. The oil crisis has taken decades to transpire, supplies are limited, and we are approaching precarious times. Yet consumption is only accelerating.

There is a sequence of five things you can do to avoid being the proverbial dead frog. To get ready, turn a piece of paper horizontally. Draw a line from one side to the other. Put a dot in the middle and write the word "today" above it.

First, identify signposts. Put the last ten years of your life on a time line. Identify all the defining moments, turning points, life markers, and even advances in technology that have impacted you directly.

Second, identify feelings. What feelings do you associate with these signposts? List these feelings over each signpost. You can have two paradoxical feelings over one signpost, for example, freedom and complexity.

Third, identify trends. The signposts and feelings will reveal trends. How have you made decisions in the past? Do you wait until everything goes wrong before you change course? What feelings keep popping up? Do you want to keep feeling those feelings?

Fourth, identify the next signposts. Use your imagination and inner desires to identify signposts for the next ten years. What defining moments, turning points, life markers, and other things can you identify that you guess will impact you in the next decade?

Fifth, identify feelings you want to have. Simple enough. Choose the future you want to feel.

Okay, before you carry on with your day, take fifteen minutes and do this exercise. This brief investment in yourself will keep you out of the soup (so to speak).

62 | REINVENT OR FINE-TUNE

How did Green Day fine-tune and reinvent themselves?

Listen to Green Day's 1999 CD *Nimrod* and you will hear a punk band's attempt at music. The music had a following, but piercing and tattoos were the dress code and sixty dollars of your paycheck went directly to your weekly hair gel budget.

Listen to Green Day's latest CD, *American Idiot*, and you'll hear a pop band's gold mine of four number-one hit singles.

What did Billie Joe Armstrong and his band Green Day do differently?

They fine-tuned their skills and reinvented themselves.

Joe Calloway had a successful speaking business. One day, he threw out everything and changed lanes to a message on branding. After two best-selling books (*A Category of One* and *Indisputable*) it is difficult to for meeting planners to get Joe at their meetings because he is already in high demand.

What did Joe do differently?

He fine-tuned his expertise and reinvented himself.

BlueCoat Systems was on the threshold of going out of business. They stood at a public company's equivalent of death's door. In three short years the leadership responded to a need in the market and courageously charged ahead with a new solution. Today their stock is trading at $40.18 and they are in the throes of a new initiative that would create explosive growth.

What did BlueCoat do differently?

They didn't have the luxury of fine-tuning, and immediately reinvented themselves.

What merit could you see in fine-tuning and/or reinventing yourself?

Here are three things you can do:

1. **Throw out the old stuff you're hanging on to.** By tossing the stuff that has lost its sizzle for you and your customers, you open up space for new stuff that generates interest.

2. **Analyze the market and match your findings with what you are passionate about.** What is your market desperate

for? What solutions do they need? What does the customer of your customer want? What things strike a chord with the things that you are passionate about?

3. **Reinvention is all about timing.** Fine-tuning will be your important first step. Reinvention is part of a process of analysis and fine-tuning. But when it is time to reinvent, then an informed decision and courage are important determinants.

63| SIX SIGMA KILLS INNOVATION

Chaos, disruption, freestyle decision-making, and ready-fire-aim will unlock a few doors to new opportunity.

Six Sigma, the shining beacon of efficiency and corporate nirvana, has the potential to kill innovation.

Systems and processes are key to the success of a corporation, but they are not the only key. Chaos, disruption, freestyle decision-making, and "ready-fire-aim" will unlock a few doors to new opportunity.

Here are three ways to ensure Six Sigma doesn't kill innovation at your company.

Protect the crazies. I asked Bill Perez, former CEO of S.C. Johnson and Nike, about innovation and he said, "I must protect the crazies." He knew the heart of innovation would come outside of the system. The crazies, as Perez put it, are people who don't fit it. They are the people who think differently.

Reduce, eliminate, raise, and create. At every strategy meeting that you hold, ask yourself what business factors you would reduce, eliminate, raise, and create. In Kim and Mauborgne's book *Blue Ocean Strategy* it is explained that competing more efficiently in your current market space is not the sole answer. Listing the business factors that you can reduce, eliminate, increase, and create will uncover innovative directions to take your company into uncontested market space.

Hire ignorant consultants. Why would you only hire consultants that are familiar with your industry? To hear the things you want to hear? Hire consultants who have a successful track record but know nothing about your industry. Hire thinkers. Hire people who listen. Hire speed-skiing Olympians of questionable sanity who write about ways to transform personal and workplace performance . . . (Too much? Too obvious?)

Listen . . . I like Six Sigmatians. They're nice, well-meaning people. Just keep a leash on these critters or they might kill all that is holy in our corporate cathedral . . . the innovators.

64| JUDGING BABIES

To make the most of new ideas, listen, question, and clarify.

"You don't judge a baby by his table manners."

—*Christie Hefner, president and CEO, Playboy Media Corporation*

Hefner was referring to the importance of nurturing new ideas, not shooting them down. Leaders interested in growing and evolving their organizations should take heed instead of finding fault, then dismissing a new idea. Give new ideas a chance to mature and evolve. They may surprise you.

To make the most of new ideas, follow the ABCs of LQC:

A. **Listen.** Don't be one of those leaders who think they must have all the answers. Don't be the person who is waiting for a break in the conversation to insert what she wants to say next. Instead, listen carefully and deliberately. Put judgment aside and just take in the ideas you hear.

B. **Question.** There is no quicker way to extinguish the potential of a new idea than by making a statement instead of asking a question. Positive or negative statements can have a nullifying effect. Judging new ideas as good or bad cuts short any prospects of idea-evolution. Ask questions that encourage input, accountability, and analytical thinking.

C. **Clarify.** Clarify, don't assume. Double-check that what you hear is what is being said. Repeat clarification as necessary.

Do all this and you may still find the idea stinks. If so, change the idea-diaper and repeat the ABCs of LQC.

65| SUNDIALS IN THE SHADE

Wasted strengths are powerful adversaries to well-run organizations.

Your company can make more profit! And you, my friend, are the solution. Capitalize on your strengths and everything will improve. You will be a hero and gain job security all at once!

Easier said than done.

In a Gallup survey of over 1.7 million people, in 101 companies, in 63 countries, only 20 percent of employees working in large organizations said they predominantly do what they do best. Even more astonishing, the higher a person climbs in an organization, the less likely he is to use his strengths.

According to authors Marcus Buckingham and Donald Clifton in *Now, Discover Your Strengths*, "Most organizations remain startlingly inefficient at capitalizing on the strengths of their people." There is an "unrealized capacity that resides in every single employee."

Wasted strengths are a powerful adversary to well-run organizations. Put more graphically, wasted strengths, in the words of Benjamin Franklin, are like "sundials in the shade."

There are three steps you can take to properly illuminate your strengths or the strengths of your people.

1. **Step back.** Take a system-based look at what your strengths may be. Use a self-discovery tool like an advanced learning and coaching system to shed direct light on you or your people. Find out what really makes people tick and you discover a wealth of opportunity.

2. **Step sideways.** If your job feels like a hamster wheel, your best option might be to step off. Clearly it takes courage to take a new course. For example, after acquiring a degree in economics and a cubicle on a massive New York office floor, Chris Lattanzio took a step sideways. Expression in a unique form of art was his passion. After years of unfaltering dedication to his strengths, Lattanzio now sells his art for thousands of dollars and was selected as the official artist for the Olympic Winter Games in Torino, Italy.

If you are a manager with a struggling employee, heed the words of Peter Drucker, "To keep misfits in jobs they cannot do is not being kind; it's being cruel." (Note: Stepping sideways does not necessarily mean firing or quitting. A new role in the organization may be exactly what's needed.)

3. **Step wisely.** Once you identify and execute on the things that you love to do and are great at, accelerate growth by managing your steps. Prudently balance your weaker performance activities through delegation, limitation, or elimination. Power ahead with what jazzes you up and you will ultimately reap rewards beyond your expectations.

It takes resolute courage to take any one of these three steps. With courage, you can take your sundial out of the shade and enjoy the time of your life.

66| PICK THE SMART LINE

Pick the fastest and best line to your destination: identify the straight line, identify the detours line, identify the smart line.

Staring down the slope of the world's longest speed-skiing track pulls your focus into acute clarity. Picking your line is a decision about your best guess on the fastest, most naturally efficient path to your destination. The sound of the other competitors, your breathing and even your heartbeat disappear. The only thing on your mind is the line you have chosen and how fast you can possibly go.

In business today, there are a multitude of things that can happen and you know they will come at you fast. So, the line you choose is of utmost importance.

Here is how to pick the fastest and best line to your destination:

First identify the straight line. Define the shortest distance between you and the outcome you desire. For example, let's say you want to close a deal and you know that going straight to the decision maker is the straight line.

$$You \longrightarrow \text{Decision Maker} \longrightarrow \text{Closing the Deal}$$

Second identify the detours line. Imagine all points that could take you closer (or keep you away) from the outcome you want. Pinpoint all the people who can influence the decision maker. Also research all the issues that the decision maker might be dealing with. With google.com and an imagination you can find all sorts of issues the company might be struggling with.

Third identify the smart line. Collect information that will lead you to the heart of the solution. Then draw the most efficient and effective line to the outcome you desire. In the case of closing the deal, you can see how this works. Interview one key person who is an influencer to the decision maker. This person would have a handle on the issues that are on the mind of the decision maker. Let's say the executive assistant is the influencer. You ask the EA for help. With the issues you have already researched, you clearly state that you have ideas but didn't want to bother the decision maker until you were sure you had the right solution. The influencer fills you in and becomes a partner in the solution. You are then ready to go to the decision maker.

The "smart line" might not be the most direct path. But when it's well thought out, you will likely triumph with speed and fearless clarity.

67 | GREAT COMPANY, GREAT STRATEGY (PART 1)

Finding the right strategy for success is more than valuable, it is essential.

ALERT! The odds are you will be out of business in ten years. Statistics show that only eighteen out of one hundred businesses ever make it to the ten-year mark. Each year eight hundred thousand businesses fail. Therefore, finding the right strategy for success is more than valuable, it is essential. What are you doing to beat the odds?

There are three basic company types that make the above statistics possible. First, there are those that are running the race but have no idea how far behind they are. Others struggle with developing the organization while trying to keep up with a rapidly changing marketplace. Lastly, there are front-running companies who are shining examples of high performance in the workplace.

Behind every great company is a great strategy. Great strategies are inevitably influenced by a compelling vision. Developing a vision-minded acronym can effectively help focus a mission statement to resonate better with your workforce. With relevant words, this acronym will resonate first with your internal customer (your employees), then your external customer (the people who want to give you their money).

For example, Weisman Enterprises, Inc. follows the principle in its acronym SOAR (Supportive, Objective, Accountable, Responsive). In a like manner, Audi sells car buyers the "ultimate Audi experience" with the PURE (Personal Unique Responsive Experience) system. Also, the chances are good that while you read this article there is a coach somewhere in North America saying, "TEAM, Together Each Achieves More!" Acronyms are everywhere. How can you best use them?

68| GREAT COMPANY, GREAT STRATEGY (PART 2)

Developing a vision-minded acronym can effectively help focus a mission statement to resonate better with your workforce.

Let's take a closer look at one of the examples from the previous section. At the heart of the Weisman Enterprises strategy are guiding principles for each employee. These principles are outlined in the acronym SOAR:

SUPPORTIVE—Assist and encourage others in pursuing their values and dreams

OBJECTIVE—Accurate observation and honest feedback resulting in unbiased decision-making

ACCOUNTABLE—Ownership and acceptance of actions, accomplishments and shortcomings

RESPONSIVE—Timely action in addressing needs and requests

Weisman Enterprises states, "SOAR represents behaviors, attitudes, and systems within Weisman Enterprises. It's more than a philosophy; it's our soul. It's how we do business—internally and externally. SOAR aims to maintain stability and longevity for Weisman Enterprises, our clients, our supply partners, and the community at large. We achieve this by developing relationships of loyalty, trust, and commitment."

69| GREAT COMPANY, GREAT STRATEGY (PART 3)

The Audi PURE acronym: Personal, Unique, Responsive, Experience

Let's take a closer look at one more example. Audi North America's sales force uses the acronym PURE: "It's a whole new approach to providing the ultimate Audi experience." PURE is:

PERSONAL—When you tailor each experience to meet the needs of your customer, you provide something that goes beyond the product.

UNIQUE—When your actions and ideas are innovative and unexpected, your customers recognize there's something unique about Audi. Something they cannot find anywhere else.

RESPONSIVE—When you interact and respond to your customers with the attention they desire, you establish long and lasting relationships.

EXPERIENCE—The positive experiences you provide for your customers help them become Audi advocates and results in an ownership experience they look forward to repeating.

You can see how acronyms can be a great tool for conveying your company mission and vision.

70| ACCOUNTABILITY IN THE WORKPLACE: IT'S IN THE MIX (PART 1)

Being accountable and taking responsibility is a key to success in our competitive times.

When employees are part of the solution they lead by example. Being accountable and taking responsibility is a key to success in our competitive times.

"Postal service," "happily married," and "Microsoft Works"; all terms cynics are likely to classify as oxymorons. With the ever-increasing self-absorbtion in today's society, the term "accountability in the workplace" may well deserve the same label. Mix this with aging baby boomers, who generally want to finish up their responsibilities and retire, together with Generation Xers, who appreciate only instant gratification. You now have a recipe for widespread victim mentality, not accountability. The challenge facing leadership today is finding ways to establish a healthier, accountable mentality.

Robert F. Kennedy often quoted George Bernard Shaw with "Some men see things as they are and say 'Why?' I dream things that never were, and say 'Why not?'" It is this shift that leaders need to inspire in their employees. Plus, the leaders themselves need to harvest a new culture best defined by Richard Beckhard: "Truly effective leaders in the years ahead will have personas determined by strong values and belief in the capacity of individuals to grow." When individuals have a commitment to personal growth, they have accountability. When the values of an organization are unshakable, a culture of trust where each person carries the torch of progress is created.

What ingredients are necessary for individual and workplace accountability?

Like any good recipe, there are main ingredients and flavor ingredients. To create a culture of individual and workplace accountability, you need two main ingredients, practical magic and values. And, for flavor, a dash of education.

71 | ACCOUNTABILITY IN THE WORKPLACE: DON'T FORGET THE MAGIC (PART 2)

Adding practical magic as a key ingredient to the leadership mix sets up a culture of individual and organizational accountability.

There are certain ingredients necessary for individual and workplace accountability.

Let's explore the Practical Magic.

In 1984, Michael Eisner took over as chairman and CEO of the Walt Disney Company. Prior to 1984, Disney was a company of family movies and a profitable theme park. Since that time Eisner helped build a massive $23 billion empire with blockbuster movies, ownership of ABC, ESPN, three movie studios, two cruise ships, three immense theme parks, and two more parks destined for Japan and China.

Eisner maintains that in good times and bad, he leads by four main tenants.

1. Being an example
2. Being there
3. Being a nudge and
4. Being an idea generator

Eisner's first leadership principle is the most important. Leadership by example starts at the top. As each level of the hierarchy picks up on this quality each of the subordinate levels (in theory) will follow suit. Blanketing this leadership approach Eisner wants to "make sure people throughout the organization routinely perform practical magic—a potent mix of exciting ideas and hardheaded questioning." By adding practical magic as a key ingredient to the leadership mix, Eisner has set up a culture blending individual and organizational accountability.

Next we'll explore another key ingredient: values.

72| ACCOUNTABILITY IN THE WORKPLACE: THE ROLE OF VALUES (PART 3)

The organization and the individual both need to embrace a culture of accountability.

Let's look at the role of values in accountability.

Old habits die hard. In a hierarchical structure, each level naturally seeks to justify its existence. In a way, this could be thought of as being accountable. But the definition of accountability for effective operations in the twenty-first century has to change for the individual and the organization. This is a tall order given the lack of loyalty individuals and organizations are creating for each other. As a result, the foundational basis for success is a commitment to a strong set of defined values—both individually and organizationally—and the alignment of shared values.

If the organization involves the individual employees in an awareness of the corporate values and a process of understanding how they align with personal values, both will embrace new levels of accountability and achieve success.

The organization and the individual need to both embrace a culture of accountability. The organization must trust the individual to grow and learn. The individual must honor that trust and apply his or her values for the good of the organization. If either side fails to meet its half of the bargain all will suffer.

Next we'll explore another key ingredient: a dash of education.

73 | ACCOUNTABILITY IN THE WORKPLACE: A DASH OF EDUCATION (PART 4)

We are well on our way to perfecting a recipe for a culture that understands the value of constantly improving and being accountable for our results.

The flavor in this recipe is a dash of education.

I've discovered several ways to build accountability through education in my own company by setting up three key mechanisms:

1. **Support for personal and professional growth.** I trust the individual knows what areas he or she needs to work on. I offer to pay half of the cost of a course or educational opportunity. The individual thinks twice before requesting a course since his money is at stake, too. Plus, an employee investing his or her own money naturally has an increased commitment in gaining something from the educational experience.

2. **Here's your rope.** This means "Go out there and see what you can accomplish. If you hang yourself, together we'll figure out what went wrong." I want my people to know they have enough rope necessary to discover opportunities for the organization. Truth be known, most of the time, what an employee does is not exactly how I would have done it. Yet the return on investment of my overall trust is a more loyal, happy, involved, and accountable employee.

3. **Staged feedback.** This is a process I found works wonders for defining accountability. For the companies I own, we use several feedback mechanisms including a three-day planning, strategy, and team-building retreat as a first stage. The second stage occurs over the balance of the year in our weekly staff meeting. The agenda has a personal and professional flavor to it. We discuss organizational advancement, hot topics, and personal growth. These two stages help bond the group and have allowed us to retain loyal and proactive people.

Of course we still struggle with organizational and individual accountability like most organizations. But I feel we are well on our way to perfecting a recipe for a culture that understands the value of constantly improving and being accountable for our results.

74 | **LEAKY ROOFS**

Leaders may know that their company has to change course, but it rarely happens until there is a sustained pain in the bottom line.

"The time to repair the roof is when the sun is shining."

—JFK

What is it about human nature that we have to wait to be uncomfortable before we change our situation?

Pain is the x factor.

Pain is a powerful motivator. If you have pain in your life, you will do most anything to get rid of it. The bigger the pain, the bigger the motivation to fix it.

Leaders may know that their company has to change course but it rarely happens until there is a sustained pain in the bottom line.

Some people can be a sustained pain in the bottom line. Yet we keep them around until the discomfort is so great we get rid of the source of the pain.

There are health pains. But do we do the back exercises to strengthen the core to prevent back pain? Nooooo. People like you and I have to wait until we have a back spasm in the back yard and wait four hours lying on the ground, unable to move, before someone finds us. The pain is so great that we finally get the surgery.

So, what to do?

Preempt the pain. Take action on this sunny day. Don't wait for it to rain again. Fix the proverbial "leaky roof" now!

Predict the pain. List off all the painful consequences of waiting it out and putting off the inevitable. Imagine for a few seconds how each one would feel if it were happening in your life.

Prescribe the pain. If you're so hard-headed that you need to feel pain before you take action, then get it over with. Confront a situation or person that is the source of the pain. Get in the middle of it and then get yourself out. But *don't* ignore it!

No one wants to be, *or have,* a pain in his bottom line.

Take action now!

75 | REST FOR THE WEARY

It's hard to feel weary when you take a moment to balance your activities, reward your efforts, rejuvenate, and rest.

I was asked recently what one word I would use to describe the audiences I speak to . . .

The answer was "weary."

Sound familiar?

A National Institute for Occupational Safety and Health study revealed that 40 percent of all workers today reported feelings of being overworked and pressured to the point of depression, anxiety, and disease. The American Institute for Stress (AIS) estimates 60 percent of doctor visits are from stress-related grievances.

And how are the companies managing?

AIS estimates American businesses are losing around $300 billion annually (ebidda-ebidda-ebidda-I said . . . $300 *billion* per year) to absenteeism, reduced productivity, health care and other costs related to stress. The Henry J. Kaiser Family Foundation reports that health insurance premiums outpaced inflation fourfold to 11.2 percent in 2004.

Companies are getting a tad weary too.

Clues to solving this weariness can be found at your local playground:

1. **The seesaw.** Perfect balance is unrealistic. Yet treat balance as a dynamic exchange of forces and you are on to something. For every pressure circumstance you experience, engage in activities without pressure. Meditation is the most effective tool. Much like a seesaw, it is the exchange of force on one side and counterinfluence on the other side that makes life a fulfilling experience. In the meantime, just pray Hefty Boy doesn't ruin the fun with an I'm-gonna-keep-you-in-the-air-for-as-long-as-I-like stunt.

2. **The slide.** Speaking of rewarding, for every climb you undertake, be sure to reward yourself with something fun. Climb up, sit down, put your arms in the air, scootch ahead, and yell "weeeeeeeeeeee." Climb again and repeat until dark.

3. **The jungle gym.** Getting up the jungle gym can be tricky. It takes careful concentration and execution. Yet, reach the top and what's left to do but sit down and enjoy the view? You work hard. Take a moment now and then and sit by a lake, walk in nature, zone out in a movie, get on the floor and

color with a child, do something that is a break from all that concentrating.

Now, how do you feel?

Hard to feel weary when you take a moment to dynamically balance your activities, reward your efforts, rejuvenate, and rest now and then.

Also by Vince Poscente:

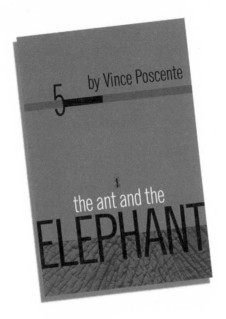

The Ant and the Elephant

A different kind of book for a different kind of leader!
A great story that teaches that we must lead ourselves
before we can expect to be an effective leader of others.

Soft cover $12.95
Hard cover $19.95

Inspirational Quotes from *The Ant and the Elephant*

"Before you can become a great leader to
others, you first must understand yourself."

———

"Life should be a fulfilling journey,
not just a struggle to survive."

———

"Without conflict there is no growth,
and the most challenging conflict is within ourselves."

———

"We live in a world of instant gratification,
but we need to fight that pressure and remember
that the worthiest goals take time and energy."

———

"A goal with a depth of meaning has an emotional buzz."

———

"Inspire your team through emotion.
Never underestimate the power of emotion."

———

"The power within, aligned with the power of the many,
is equivalent to a tiny ant guiding a mighty elephant."

———

"Shift beliefs, attitudes and truths
so they are aligned with your vision."

———

"Envision *having* the goal rather
than merely *wanting* the goal."

———

"Experience the goal as though
it were happening right now."

———

"Gratitude is the magic ingredient in the recipe
for a fulfilling life."

———

"Zero in on a goal that has a depth of meaning.
The journey has to be worth taking."

Accelerate Personal Growth

12 Choices…That Lead to Your Success is about success – how to achieve it, keep it and enjoy it – by making better choices. **$14.95**

Orchestrating Attitude translates the abstract into the actionable. This book cuts through the clutter to deliver inspiration and application so you can orchestrate your attitude … and your success. **$9.95**

107 Ways to Stick to It Learn the secrets from the world's highest achievers. These practical tips and inspiring stories will help you stick to it and WIN! **$9.95**

The Ant and the Elephant is a great story that teaches that we must lead ourselves before we can expect to be an effective leader of others. **$12.95**

175 Ways to Get More Done in Less Time has 175 really good suggestions that will help you get things done faster … and usually better. **$9.95**

136 Effective Presentation Tips provides you with inside tips from two of the best presenters in the world. **$9.95**

You and Your Network is profitable reading for those who want to learn how to develop healthy relationships with others. **$9.95**

Becoming the Obvious Choice is a roadmap showing each employee how they can maintain their motivation, develop their talents and become the best. **$9.95**

Too Many Emails contains dozens of tips and techniques to increase your email effectiveness and efficiency. **$9.95**

Conquering Adversity – Six Strategies to Move You and Your Team Through Tough Times is a practical guide to help people and organizations deal with the unexpected and move forward through adversity. **$14.95**

The CornerStone Perpetual Calendar, a compelling collection of quotes about leadership and life, is perfect for office desks, school and home. **$14.95**

CornerStone Collection of Note Cards Sampler Pack is designed to make it easy for you to show appreciation for your team, clients and friends. The awesome photography and your personal message written inside will create a lasting impact. Pack of 12 (one each of all 12 designs) **$24.95**

Visit www.CornerStoneLeadership.com for additional books and resources.

Order Form

1-30 copies $14.95   31-100 copies $13.95   101+ copies $12.95

Silver Bullets   _____ copies X _____ = $ _____

Additional Personal Growth Resources

Accelerate Personal Growth Package   _____ pack(s) X $139.95 = $ _____
(Includes one copy of *Silver Bullets* and one
of each item listed on the previous page.)

Other Books

_____   _____ copies X _____ = $ _____

_____   _____ copies X _____ = $ _____

_____   _____ copies X _____ = $ _____

                                  Shipping & Handling $ _____

                                             Subtotal $ _____

                            Sales Tax (8.25%-TX Only) $ _____

                            Total (U.S. Dollars Only) $ _____

Shipping and Handling Charges

Total $ Amount	Up to $49	$50-$99	$100-$249	$250-$1199	$1200-$2999	$3000+
Charge	$6	$9	$16	$30	$80	$125

Name _____ Job Title _____

Organization _____ Phone _____

Shipping Address _____ Fax _____

Billing Address _____ Email _____

City _____ State _____ ZIP _____

❏ Please invoice (Orders over $200) P.O.# (if applicable) _____

Charge Your Order: ❏ MasterCard   ❏ Visa   ❏ American Express

Credit Card Number _____ Exp. Date _____

Signature _____

❏ Check Enclosed (Payable to: CornerStone Leadership)

Mail

Phone 888.789.5323   **P.O. Box 764087**
Fax 972.274.2884   www.**CornerStoneLeadership**.com   **Dallas, TX 75376**

Thank you for reading *Silver Bullets*.
We hope it has assisted you in your quest for
personal and professional growth.

CornerStone Leadership is committed to provide new
and enlightening products to organizations worldwide.
Our mission is to fuel knowledge with practical resources
that will accelerate your team's productivity,
success and job satisfaction!

Best wishes for your continued success.

CornerStone
Leadership Institute
www.CornerStoneLeadership.com

*Start a crusade in your organization –
have the courage to learn, the vision to lead,
and the passion to share.*